Profit vs. Progress

Profit vs. Progress

Why Socially Responsible Investment Doesn't Work and How to Fix It

Brad Swanson

The MIT Press
Cambridge, Massachusetts
London, England

The MIT Press
Massachusetts Institute of Technology
77 Massachusetts Avenue
Cambridge, MA 02139
mitpress.mit.edu

The MIT Press would like to thank the anonymous peer reviewers who provided comments on drafts of this book. The generous work of academic experts is essential for establishing the authority and quality of our publications. We acknowledge with gratitude the contributions of these otherwise uncredited readers.

This book was set in ITC Stone Serif Std and ITC Stone Sans Std by New Best-set Typesetters Ltd. Printed and bound in the United States of America.

Library of Congress Cataloging-in-Publication Data is available.

ISBN: 978-0-262-05159-0

10 9 8 7 6 5 4 3 2 1

EU Authorised Representative: Easy Access System Europe, Mustamäe tee 50, 10621 Tallinn, Estonia | Email: gpsr.requests@easproject.com

To Anne
Without whom it would not have been possible

Contents

Preface

I've been thinking about this book for a long time.

Early in my career, while serving as an American diplomat in several African countries, I saw firsthand the limitations of foreign assistance in helping poor countries develop their economies. Several years later, after leaving the Foreign Service and becoming an investment banker, I revisited my first overseas post, Senegal. There I advised the government on selling the state-owned telecoms network to a global player with ample capital to invest. I think I did more good the second time around than the first.

I love capitalism. There is nothing more innovative and productive than self-interest. Freely competitive markets generate enormous amounts of wealth.

But my love is not unconditional. I know the pitfalls of capitalism. Left alone, the wealth it generates flows increasingly uphill. In the absence of firm guiderails, capitalism locks into a self-reinforcing system of oppression. While affluence builds at the top, misery deepens at the bottom, and the environment and the climate are collateral damage.

This is where we are today. But the socially responsible finance industry tells us it is doing its part—delivering, simultaneously, market-rate investment returns and world-bettering social and environmental value. The industry has grown into a multitrillion-dollar powerhouse on the back of promising that we can have it all. The main point of this book is to say it's not so.

I am part of that industry, as a socially responsible fund manager. At least I work in a corner of the market, impact investing, where most investors understand the notion of a trade-off of financial for social returns. But even on my home turf, there is a lot of misunderstanding—some of it willful.

The more I thought about this book, the simpler its messages became. There are only three—simple, but with serious implications.

First, most of what sustainable finance promises is empty—and if you have investments in its worst parts, you should let them go.

Second, this is not a moral issue. The markets work as they are designed to do, and most people in sustainable finance, like most people everywhere, are honorable—even if they are inadvertently worsening problems instead of solving them.

Third, if we want the outcome of the game to change—if we want companies to be more socially responsible—we have to change the rules. And that means legislation, not investment.

I think you will be surprised to learn how sustainable finance spins its illusory web. Maybe angry at how it damages society at large, not just unsuspecting investors. But mostly, I hope you will be energized—to support a political movement to revise the rulebook, as we have done before, so that capital can flow more freely to where it will do the most good.

Introduction: What Is Socially Responsible Investment?

If you could improve environmental and social problems by investing in companies that make the world better while still earning market-rate financial returns, wouldn't you do it?

This is the promise underlying an investment strategy called environmental, social, and governance—ESG for short—that has swept the world, accumulating about $30 trillion of assets under management, or about a quarter of the global total.[1]

We are all invested in ESG, directly or indirectly. Many of us have stakes in mutual funds following ESG guidelines. In addition, the banks that hold our deposits, the insurance companies that pay our claims, the pension funds that provide our retirement income—most maintain a portion of their assets in ESG securities.

But what is ESG? Most people who have heard of it think that ESG measures corporate social responsibility. They see it as a holistic assessment of a company's contribution to the well-being of not just shareholders but all "stakeholders," including employees, customers, suppliers, the communities in which it operates, the environment, and society at large. Companies with high ESG ratings are assumed to be social benefactors to the world.

In a survey of retail investors, more than three-quarters, 77 percent, said that companies held in an ESG fund aligned with their values, while 63 percent disagreed with the statement that a company's role is to maximize earnings, not pursue social or environmental goals.[2]

But how many of those in the survey had examined ESG closely? In fact, they were looking through the wrong end of the telescope. ESG is asset management, not social activism. The only stakeholder whose interest ESG takes into account is the shareholder.

Yes, ESG analyzes social and environmental risks but only those that could significantly affect a company's financial performance—that is, shareholder value. ESG's mission is not to save the world. It is to deliver market-rate or better returns by favoring companies adept at dealing with threats to their profitability posed by the environmental and social problems they face in their businesses.

To understand what this means in practice, consider the most antisocial industry imaginable: cigarettes. The products kill the customers. Surely, the ESG rating of tobacco companies is zero?

Well, no. Cigarette makers typically achieve ESG ratings in the middle of the pack (so to speak), high enough that some ESG funds invest in them.

How can this be? Because smoking is legal, and cigarette makers rarely face substantial liability for the death it causes. The harm that comes from cigarettes doesn't appear on the balance sheets of the tobacco companies. Therefore, it does not count for much in ESG ratings.

There are, certainly, some environmental and social risks that could affect the cigarette companies' bottom line. For example, tobacco is a thirsty crop and depletes the soil. In addition, like other manufacturers, cigarette makers are concerned with issues like workplace safety and employee turnover.

By dealing relatively effectively with these sorts of risks, cigarette companies can achieve respectable ESG ratings and enter into stock portfolios—where they add significant investment value, since their customers are addicted and will keep buying at any cost. (This is a tragic example of what economists coldly call "price insensitivity.") This also benefits ESG fund managers since, like other fund managers, they earn higher fees from higher financial returns.

Similarly, fossil fuel companies—also typically high earners—often obtain decent ESG ratings, so 80 percent of ESG funds invest in them despite their role in bringing about climate catastrophe.[3] Big Oil is not charged for the damage that its carbon dioxide (CO_2) emissions inflict on the world.

Casinos, junk food producers, liquor manufacturers—many companies whose products can ruin lives boast superior ESG scores and appear prominently in ESG portfolios.

ESG financing does not prod companies to be better social performers, since it only deals with issues that risk managers should be aware of in any case, as they are financially material, by definition. If a company thinks its profits will rise by switching to renewable power, or by improving its employees' benefits, it will do so, whether or not ESG takes notice. By only including risks that already appear on the company's agenda, ESG is a cheerleader, not a player.

But the hypocrisy of ESG goes deeper. Most ESG funds attempt to generate market-rate returns for their investors by tracking the performance of a general market index. However, that means their portfolios look very similar to the index, and hence the ESG scores of those portfolios are also quite close. An ESG fund is hard to distinguish from a market fund, except in one respect—it usually charges higher fees.

Although it is by far the largest form of "socially responsible investment" (SRI)—the general term for investing with both social and financial objectives—ESG is not the only SRI investment style. (Note that SRI and "sustainable investment" are used synonymously now, although "sustainable" originally had more of an environmental overtone.)

Besides ESG, the other large focus of SRI, sometimes overlapping with ESG, is "climate finance"—investments aimed at reducing global warming, directly or indirectly. Climate finance is as problematic as ESG. Big corporations that commit to achieving "net-zero" emissions rarely follow through, the evidence shows. Investor alliances dedicated to facilitate the climate transition through their financing policies do not practice what they preach. And voluntary "carbon offsets"—projects meant to compensate for carbon emissions, like reforestation or solar energy—is a market rife with phony deals.

Even "green bonds," the most dynamic area of climate finance, are green in name only. Green bonds are debt securities whose proceeds are used for environmental projects, like renewable energy. The market for green bonds is large ($3 trillion[4]) and liquid. Green bonds owe their popularity in large part to the common perception that they facilitate green projects. But in financial terms, they don't.

Green bonds customarily have the same risk standing as general-purpose bonds from the same issuer. Because bond buyers accept the same risk of default on the green bond as on the issuer's other bonds, they require the same yield. And because of this, the projects funded with green bonds must generate the same return on investment as any of the bond issuer's other projects. If not, the issuer might have difficulty repaying the bond. Since green bonds are economically equivalent to the issuers' other bonds, they do not make green projects any more attractive financially.

What we mostly see in SRI, whether in ESG or climate finance, is the finance industry holding up a big sign advertising social and environmental value, behind which they conduct business as usual. Investors seek market-rate returns, and companies strive to maximize shareholder value. The trade-off of financial for social performance is ignored, or even denied.

The exception to this is "impact investing," a sector that does put social objectives ahead of, or on a par with, financial ones. But it only accounts for about $1 trillion of investment,[5] 3 percent the size of ESG, as companies on the social side of the social-financial trade-off tend to be smaller and riskier than those on the other side, and deliver below-market investment returns.

The structure of the finance industry, not moral weakness, is to blame for SRI's failure to stimulate greater corporate social responsibility. Most of the capital in the stock market, about 80 percent,[6] is managed by institutional money managers. Many of them are under a legal obligation, called "fiduciary duty," requiring them to act in the best interests of their clients. This is usually interpreted as aiming for the best financial returns available within specified risk parameters.

An institutional investor, like a pension fund, that invested in companies with high social performance but subpar profitability could be accused of breaching their fiduciary duty—and might even run the risk of being unable to honor its obligations.

We should not forget that these are commercial enterprises, competing for capital and wanting to show that they can produce investment returns as good as, or better than, their peers. Whether fiduciaries or not, the business of asset managers is making money for their clients.

Nor can we fault companies for prioritizing financial returns over social ones. In free markets, companies have to compete to attract capital. The stock exchange does not reward companies for serving other stakeholders unless shareholders benefit as well.

True, long-term profitability might improve if corporations upped their social responsibility game. Operating conditions would be more propitious in a world without climate warming and social injustice.

But the deck is stacked against corporate farsightedness. Directors on the board who don't maximize proximate value for shareholders run the risk of being fired by them. In addition, stock prices respond more to short-term earnings forecasts than long-range ones.[7] One reason for this is that projections are more uncertain the farther out they venture. A bigger reason is that money managers are rewarded for quarterly, or even monthly, performance.

Once economic arguments are exhausted, civic virtue is the last refuge of the social investment advocate. After all, aren't corporations people, too—or at least managed by them? Even at some financial cost, executives should be good citizens and embody loftier goals than mere shareholder returns in their leadership.

But in practice, psychology tells us, organizations, including companies, often form tight communities whose members, consciously or not, subordinate personal values in the common quest to achieve strategic goals. "Groupthink" can lead to behavior and outcomes, validated by the group, that individual members might recoil from in a different context.[8]

In our capitalist system, the government has traditionally acted as the counterweight to shareholder value, changing the parameters when the imbalances inherent in free markets threatened to cause irreparable harm. Far from handicapping corporations, the reforms of the Progressive Era and the New Deal left them more dynamic than before.

Today we are again at an inflection point, with income inequality at worse levels than during the Gilded Age of robber barons and Dickensian poverty.[9] Socioeconomic mobility is on a decades-long decline,[10] and the future of the planet is threatened by unremitting atmospheric emissions. But rather than a battering ram for change, SRI is a bulwark of the status quo.

Instead of betting that social investment will improve corporate social behavior, we should direct our efforts toward the political process. If we want the outcome of the game to change, we have to revise the rules.

Solutions are available—but they will be found in legislative assemblies, not corporate boardrooms. And only if we make our voices heard.

Plan of the Book

Today's crisis of corporate social responsibility has deep roots. Baring those roots can teach us a great deal about how to handle our current problems. That is why we start our journey at the dawn of industrial capitalism, in a textile mill in the early 1800s. Then we visit, briefly, some other critical moments when the clash of interests between shareholders and stakeholders changed history. Next, we examine the current state of the SRI industry to show how the pieces fit together, and why it fails to deliver on its promises. We finish by outlining a package of reforms that could better align free markets with greater environmental and social justice.

I Does a Corporation Have a Conscience?

1 A Lost Eden

In 1800, more than 90 percent of Americans lived on farms or in small villages in the countryside. Roads were few and transportation slow. The economy was largely decentralized. Most manufacturing took place in artisanal workshops, and most people never moved far from where they were born.

The primary basis of wealth was land. Employment was typically informal, not contractual, and most workers were not paid fixed money wages but rather received the bulk of their compensation in kind—food, finished products, agricultural commodities, and lodging.[1]

But along the banks of the Merrimack River in rural Massachusetts, a vastly different future was soon to take shape. A tight-knit group of merchants informally known as the Boston Associates traveled to England, or sent agents, to scrutinize closely the technological advances that were enabling English cloth makers to dominate the market in their former colonies.

The American entrepreneurs drew up a bold plan to mimic their British rivals and build fully integrated manufacturing plants in America for the first time. They found a suitable site with ample undeveloped land and a brisk river for power and began erecting large factories where raw cotton entered on the ground floor, rose through several stories of carding, spinning, and weaving machinery, and emerged as finished cloth at the top level.

With their hulking water wheels and long banks of clanking machines, the textile mills were a marvel in a country where most manufacturing was still done by hand and most power came from human or animal muscle. But they cost a fortune to build, and the owners were anxious to recoup their capital as early as possible.

The factories needed a large, stable, and tranquil workforce to keep the machines running. But the mills were not likely to attract the sons of New

England with their drab offering of low pay, lack of advancement, and boredom—especially as droves of young men were already abandoning the rocky soils of their family farms for fertile and cheap land in the newly opened Western territories. Compared to this dream, mill life seemed even shabbier than it was.

Young women, on the other hand, especially from lower-income families, had few opportunities to live independently. They flocked to the factories, willing to trade long hours of dull labor for a measure of social and economic autonomy that they could not hope for otherwise. The so-called mill girls who operated the looms in the town of Lowell, named after one of the largest mill owners, are the archetypal figures of the modern industrial worker.

Life was not easy for a mill girl, whose employment subjected her to the authority of the constrictive "Lowell System" set up by the mill owners. Girls as young as ten years old were employed in the textile factories, working at least twelve hours per day, six days per week. As the massive looms thundered at deafening volumes and the air filled with cotton dust, windows stayed shut and temperatures rose above ninety degrees—the better to keep the thread supple.[2]

Discipline was strict, both on and off the factory floor. The young women were required to eat and sleep—two to a bed—in cramped dormitories, owned by the mill. Their lives were regulated by bells, timetables, and detailed rules covering both work and personal life. Even a petty infraction could lead to summary dismissal.

But corporate paternalism also had a softer side. The work was long and uncomfortable but not usually debilitating or dangerous. The boarding houses restricted the young women's movements, but they provided a safe abode, three meals a day, and some common space to read, sew, converse, and even, in some boarding houses, play a piano. Free lectures and access to libraries opened vistas for learning that life on the farm lacked.

The pay was modest, especially after the mandatory deduction for room and board. But it was regular and given in cash, unlike factories in some other places that paid in scrip, which was good only for purchases at the company store, often at inflated prices. Most mill girls sent the bulk of their wages home to help families—especially their brothers' school fees—but some were able to put enough aside to lay a foundation for economic independence when they left factory work after a few years, as was customary.

"Life in the boarding-houses was very agreeable," recalled Harriet Robinson, who started work at the mills at age eleven, in 1836. The matrons "were often the friends and advisers of their boarders. Each house was a village or community of itself."[3]

In their spare time, wrote Harriet, the young women "discussed the books they read; debated religious and social questions. . . . They soon became educated far beyond what their mothers or their grandmothers could have been." On the factory floor, "their labor was monotonous and done almost mechanically, but their thoughts were free."[4]

For the mill owners, paternalism was not a gift—it was essential to their business model, with its high capital costs, dependent for profitability on consistently achieving top production levels. A reliable and low-wage workforce was intrinsic to financial success.

From the founding of the first integrated mill in 1814, the factories generated solid profits for their owners for a couple of decades. But starting in the 1830s, as mills multiplied throughout the region and technology advanced, overproduction and competition from new entrants eroded margins for the entire industry.

Fortuitously for the mill owners, waves of poor, unskilled immigrants from Ireland and elsewhere began to swell the labor force, allowing cuts in wages and higher production volumes without running short of workers. Annual dividends from the Boston Manufacturing Company, the first and one of the largest Lowell mill owners, fell from above 10 percent to 0 percent by 1842 but soon thereafter recovered and stayed at or above 5 percent for all but a few years during the remainder of the century.[5]

Meanwhile, all pretense of capitalist benevolence evaporated. In 1855, a visitor to Fall River, Massachusetts, which had grown to rival Lowell in textile production, asked a manager whether the local factories did "anything for the physical, intellectual or moral welfare of their work-people."[6]

"We never do," came the reply. "And as for myself, I regard my work-people just as I regard my machinery. So long as they can do my work for what I choose to pay them, I keep them, getting out of them all I can. . . . When my machines get old and useless, I reject them and get new, and these people are part of my machinery."[7]

Children as well as adults were part of the machinery in the Fall River mills. An official investigation into child labor in 1868 found more than a thousand children in its mills, "and these are very ignorant, some not even knowing their own ages." In one mill, an investigator uncovered "twenty-five children of both sexes employed in a basement room . . . barefooted, ill-clad, unclean and pale looking, earning very low wages."[8]

Even in Lowell itself, where the Lowell System had come to epitomize the marriage of capitalist gain and social improvement, the paternalist trappings had been largely abandoned by the 1850s.

Harriet Robinson came back to Lowell in 1882, more than forty years after her initiation as a mill girl. Now, she observed, "there was a tired hopelessness" among the young women workers she met. "They tend so many looms and frames that they have no time to think. . . . Their work was drudgery, done without aim and purpose."[9]

For Harriet, the blame lay with the manufacturers, which had turned into "soulless organization[s] . . . [whose] members forget that they are morally responsible for the souls and bodies, as well as the wages" of their workers. The industrialists should "mix a little conscience with their capital," she lamented, and bring back the "lost Eden" their workers had formerly known.[10]

2 Industrialized Serfdom

By the later years of the nineteenth century, a visitor from 1800 would have been astounded. Forty percent of Americans now lived in sprawling cities, railroads crisscrossed the land, and vast interwoven manufacturing and commercial enterprises touched the lives of all. Machines had supplanted muscles, and giant industrial plants employing thousands were turning out massive quantities of goods that moved in long trains across the landscape to markets that were no longer local but national in scope.

Wealth no longer depended on coaxing value from the soil but was mainly embodied in capital. Unlike land, which was immutable and fixed, capital could flow from a signature on a document or the tap of a telegraph key and could be transformed with infinite malleability into any of the thousands of goods and services demanded by a fast-growing and increasingly complex economy.

Capitalism provided a common language, money, for every economic act. Money also imposed a common yardstick by which the value of every exchange of one thing for another could be measured—including labor, which was now principally denominated in money wages. An intricate infrastructure of finance had developed to supply and route the rising need for capital to build factories, lay railroads, hire workers, and earn returns for capital's owners.

The rules of the game called for workers to be treated as mere costs, controlled to the greatest extent possible to give companies a competitive advantage and shareholders handsome returns. This affront to humanism was apparent from the outset, but the response of those who succeeded in the new capitalist order was to welcome it and declare it inevitable—a product of natural science.

Bolstered by false readings of Charles Darwin's novel theories of evolution, elites embraced the notion that in business, as in the jungle, "survival of the fittest" ruled, and the weak and the poor deserved contempt—or, at the most, pity—for their condition.

"Social Darwinism" was captured in its essence by, among others, railroad magnate Charles Elliott Perkins. Although (or perhaps because) he was a self-made man himself, having ascended from a humble clerk at age eighteen to the presidency of one of the nation's largest railroads—the Chicago, Burlington & Quincy—Perkins believed that capital's only obligation to labor was to encourage workers' "sobriety, industry and frugality."[1]

"That a man is entitled to a living wage is absurd," Perkins proclaimed in 1871. He continued to sound the alarm, warning a few years later that if "you take from the strong to give to the weak, you encourage weakness; therefore, let men reap what they and their progenitors sow."[2]

Disdain for the poor was complemented by reverence for the rich. "I say that you ought to get rich and it is your duty to get rich," preached Baptist Minister Russell Conwell in his immensely popular self-help book *Acres of Diamonds*, first published in 1882 (and still in print today). He continued, "Ninety-eight out of one hundred of the rich men of America are honest. That is why they are rich. . . . I sympathize with the poor, but the number of poor who are to be sympathized with is very small. . . . Let us remember there is not a poor person in the United States who was not made poor by his own shortcomings."[3]

Set against this mindset, workers could protect their interests only through collective action. Even in the early days of industrialization, the mill girls of Lowell had opposed wage cuts by walking out—twice, in 1834 and 1836. Both times the strikes failed, but over the following decades, as the capitalist transformation rolled across America, labor unions sank their roots deep into factories and along railroad lines, pushing for better pay, shorter hours, and safer working conditions.

Most industrialists saw the relationship as a zero-sum game: A dollar more to employees meant a dollar less in profits. Many did not hesitate to use deadly force against strikers. "We have machine guns, riot guns, and rifles," reported a general manager at a coal mine preparing for labor unrest. "We have tear bombs, loaded with tear gas, and we have ferry pistols . . . which shoot gas shells, and star bombs."[4]

Employers often resorted to private militias to overcome striking workers, like the Pinkerton Detective Agency, whose force of thirty thousand in

1890 was about as large as the US Army. And when their own means fell short, companies could call on local, state, or even federal armed forces to break work stoppages. Government troops were summoned to quell strikes around five hundred times between 1875 and 1910.[5]

But firepower alone could not contain the growing union movement. In the last two decades of the century, nearly 23,000 strikes took place at 117,000 company locations, many of them marked by multiple killings.[6]

Notwithstanding their desperation to ensure a compliant workforce and suppressed wages, industrialists could think no more creatively than to revive the gameplan of the Boston Associates decades earlier. In this era, however, the stakes were higher, and the scale of worker control envisaged was grander. The new principle was called "welfare work," later revised to "welfare capitalism," instead of the Lowell System, but the concept was essentially the same.

The leader of this campaign, celebrated for his vision and commitment, was George Pullman, founder and president of the Pullman Palace Car Company, the nation's largest manufacturer of railroad cars. In all he did, Pullman went big—including the creation of an entire new town, named after himself, of course, to keep workers under the company's constant supervision.

Starting in 1880, the Pullman company purchased about six square miles of undeveloped land on the outskirts of Chicago and filled it according to a detailed master plan with shops, schools, parks, a library, a theater, a hotel, and houses, where up to twelve thousand employees and family members lived.

The utopian breadth, architectural harmony, and high-level workmanship of the town of Pullman drew acclaim from many who saw in it an affirmation of the dignity of labor. But Pullman himself knew better, and spurned any notion that it was anything but a tool to create shareholder value. "Capital will not invest in sentiment, nor for sentimental considerations for the laboring class," he asserted. "But let it once be proved that enterprises of this kind are safe and profitable and we shall see great manufacturing companies develop similar enterprises, and thus a new era will be introduced in the history of labor."[7]

To prove Pullman town safe, the company owned and managed as many aspects of life as it could. No worker could own their residence; leases could be broken at the company's will; unauthorized meetings were banned; books for the library were screened; and alcohol was banned from stores to enforce, á la Charles Perkins, sobriety and frugality. To prove Pullman town profitable, the company set housing costs with a target of 6 percent return on investment. A Pullman resident summarized their lives this way: "We are born in a Pullman house, fed from the Pullman shops, taught in the Pullman school, catechized in the Pullman church, and when we die we shall go to the Pullman Hell."[8]

Like the Massachusetts mill owners, Pullman was quick to turn his back on employees when shareholder value was under fire. During an economic decline in 1893, the company cut wages for hourly workers by about 25 percent but would not consider lowering rents or utility charges. Tenants complained that the company marked up water charges five times, and three times for gas, but their pleas for relief were ignored. Meanwhile, shareholders received a dividend in 1893 and an even larger one in 1894, despite the deepening depression.[9]

With no other recourse, the workers enlisted the aid of the American Railway Union. The union requested arbitration, the company refused, and workers walked out in May 1894. The strike spread over two months to one hundred thousand workers in allied unions, and disrupted rail traffic over a large swath of the country. Ultimately, twelve thousand federal troops were deployed to crush it, at the cost of an estimated thirty deaths.

The strike was a tactical victory for the company, as workers eventually abandoned their demands and returned to the workplace, even signing a pledge not to join a union again. But it showed the limits of corporate efforts to enclose workers in a gilded cage, forcing them to collaborate in their own exploitation. Nevertheless, Pullman continued to own and operate its town until courts required the company to divest all nonindustrial holdings in 1898. Moreover, corporations continued for decades to use welfare capitalism, though not often on the scale of Pullman, as a primary weapon against union organization, alongside violence and political rhetoric.

The last word on the town of Pullman belongs to a man who probably knew it better than any other, the minister at its Methodist church, the Reverend William Carwardine. Although a man of the cloth like *Acres of Diamonds* author Conwell, he had a very different view of humanity. Rather than a workers' paradise, he viewed Pullman's creation as a "civilized relic of European serfdom."[10]

3 The Public Pushes Back

Capitalism was novel, and government was little more than a spectator to its exuberant rise. Its advocates claimed that the passivity of the state was the key to its success. In a free market system, government's role vis-à-vis business was simply to ensure general peace and stability—and the sanctity of the contract between worker and employer, no matter how unequal the balance of power between the two parties, or how unfair that contract might be in consequence.

This doctrine—known as "laissez-faire," roughly translated as "let it happen"—contended that the "invisible hand" of unchecked competition would reward efficiency and productivity and weed out substandard performers, to the ultimate benefit of all. But while unrestrained capitalism created unprecedented wealth, it concentrated that wealth in very few hands and left a large portion of the population in poverty.

In the late 1700s, on the eve of industrialization, the richest 10 percent of Americans owned less than half, about 45 percent, of the wealth of the entire nation.[1] By 1890, the top 10 percent claimed about three-quarters, 72 percent, of national wealth. Moreover, within that elite class, a tiny group of super-rich families, about four thousand of them, or 0.03 percent of the population, owned an astonishing 20 percent of overall wealth.[2] The share of the top decile overall continued to rise until it peaked at 80 percent in 1910.[3] The extravagant lifestyles of the newly wealthy at the top of society, in contrast to the grinding poverty below, led Mark Twain to describe it as a Gilded Age, and the name stuck.

Far below the glitter of the moneyed elite, the situation was dire at the base of the pyramid. In 1890, the entire bottom half of households owned only 12 percent of the nation's wealth, or less than one-quarter of their proportionate share of the pie. Within that slice, the poorest 10 percent of Americans got by, or not, with crumbs—0.4 percent of the nation's total wealth, or twenty-five times less than their pro rata share.[4]

Although poverty had not yet been defined quantitatively, contemporaries knew it when they saw it and were appalled by its prevalence in the world that capitalism had built. John Ryan began his groundbreaking book *A Living Wage* in 1906 by observing acidly that "the doctrine that every laborer has a moral right to a Living Wage is obviously in direct conflict with existing business practice and theory."[5]

Ryan, a Catholic priest and diligent researcher, was one of the first to measure income levels against the cost of living. He put together and priced a basket of goods that provided the "irreducible minimum" of basic human needs for a laborer and his family, concluding that a "living wage" in urban areas in most parts of the country was $600 per annum, though in the larger cities, like New York and Chicago, it was over $900.[6]

Since the average manufacturing wage at the time was only about $487, Ryan's research indicated that the typical industrial worker lived in deep poverty. Modern research chimes with Ryan's findings, estimating that the poverty rate in nineteenth-century American cities typically hovered around 50 percent.[7]

Besides miring industrial workers in poverty, laissez-faire capitalism led to recurrent economic crises, in which overlending and speculative investment, especially in railroads, created economic bubbles that popped suddenly and drove many businesses into bankruptcy and many workers into joblessness.

In time, the harsh reality of conspicuous consumption side by side with misery and economic volatility spurred a reevaluation of the role of government in business. Social reformers, academics, and religious figures began asserting, as part of a new movement called the "Social Gospel," that great economic power gives rise to great responsibility. One of its leaders, activist and author Jane Addams, the first American woman to win the Nobel Peace Prize, wrote, at around the time of the Pullman strike, "A large manufacturing concern has ceased to be a private matter. . . . The interests of the public are so involved that the officers of the company are in a real sense administering a public trust."[8]

But if business was to be held accountable to the public, then the state had a central role to play as the public's representative. It was time, said economist Simon Patten, who later became the chair of Wharton Business School, for "a new society, and a state whose power will be superior to that of any combination of selfish individuals, and whose duties will be commensurate with human wants."[9] In sum, said Edmund J. James, founder of the American Academy of Political and Social Science, "Government should interfere in all instances where its interference will tell for better health, better education, better morals, greater comfort of the community."[10]

The novel belief in the responsibility of government to exercise regulatory authority to better society led to a burst of legislation during 1890–1920, known as the Progressive Era. Progressivism dealt with a wide variety of topics, including immigration, land conservation, public education, liquor consumption, and voting initiatives like the direct election of US senators. But a key driver of Progressive activism was the newfound conviction that the state had a legitimate, and necessary, role to play in the interaction of business and society.

One of the Progressives' principal aims was "trust busting," breaking up corporate cartels that controlled many industries, stifling competition and stamping out innovation. The trusts' existence and operations overtly contradicted the central tenet of capitalism, free markets, but the tycoons directing them nimbly adapted their ideology, explaining that "innovation and discovery have been so busy in creating new appliances for the exploitation of the country's resources that the effective utilization of these new devices has necessitated the concentration of vast amounts of capital under the direction of a few groups of heads. As a result, we have sugar trusts, steel trusts, and combines in beef, coal, railways, and most of the other great interests."[11]

In addition, Progressives sought to stabilize the banking system, whose fragmentation and lack of transparency contributed to regularly occurring boom and bust economic cycles. They succeeded in pushing through the new Federal Reserve system despite the vigorous opposition of the "Money Trust," a small group of investment banks that exercised huge influence over large swathes of the economy through share ownership and interlocking directorships.

Upon the Fed's creation, Senator Elihu Root, whose law practice served a number of the elite members of the Money Trust, predicted an apocalypse: "We are setting our steps now in the pathway which, through the protection of a paternal government, brought the mighty power of Rome to its fall."[12]

Business leaders largely accepted the imposition of regulation in industries such as meat, food, and drugs once it became clear that Congress would not be deterred from taking action against adulterated products. They recognized that markets would be boosted by improving public confidence—moreover, smaller competitors might be forced out of business by the cost of compliance.[13]

But on some issues, business dug in its heels. For example, the leading industrial trade association, the National Association of Manufacturers (NAM), succeeded in blocking the abolition of child labor and the implementation of an eight-hour workday at the federal level, though some states took action on their own.

The NAM, and other business leaders, sought to deter Progressive reforms and cripple labor unions by rallying against what they portrayed as a new and terrifying specter: socialism. In reality, the socialist movement, calling for state ownership of the means of production, never gained much purchase in America, but it served as a convenient straw man for industrialists' self-promotion.

NAM President David Parry, speaking at his movement's annual convention in 1903, warned sternly that socialism and unionism were one: "Organized labor knows but one law, and that is the law of physical force—the law of the Huns and Vandals, the law of the savage. . . . Organized labor and the Socialist party differ in one essential respect. The former seeks to bring about socialism by forcible methods and the latter seeks the same end through the ballot box. . . . Socialism is a denial of individual and property rights, and so also is trade unionism when reduced to its last analysis."[14]

Parry was railing against a phantom. In truth, most organized labor leaders roundly rejected socialism. Here, for example, is the leading labor figure of the day, Samuel Gompers, head of the American Federation of Labor, in the same year, 1903:

> I want to tell you, Socialists, that I have studied your philosophy; read your works upon economics, and not the meanest of them; studied your standard works, both in English and German—have not only read, but studied them. I have heard your orators and watched the work of your movement the world over. I have kept close watch upon your doctrines for thirty years; have been closely associated with many of you, and know how you think and what you propose. I know, too, what you have up your sleeve. And I want to say that I am entirely at variance with your philosophy. I declare to you, I am not only at variance with your

> doctrines, but with your philosophy. Economically you are unsound; socially, you are wrong; industrially, you are an impossibility.[15]

No ambiguity here! But the manufacturers preferred to believe (or to pretend to believe) what suited their interests.

While Parry favored a headlong charge into the ranks of his enemies, other business leaders were more subtle, preferring to outflank them. Chief among these was George Perkins (not related to Charles), a leading financier who was considered a Progressive by many. He could have been mistaken for Jane Addams when he said in 1908 that "the larger the corporation becomes, the greater become its responsibilities to the entire community. The corporations of the future must be those that are semi-public servants . . . with labor so fairly and equitably treated that it will look upon its corporation as its friend."[16]

Perkins appeared to put his beliefs into practice by implementing an extensive program of welfare capitalism at US Steel, America's leading metals manufacturer. The pretense was convincing, outside the company. Still today, many cite US Steel in the early 1900s as a paragon of social responsibility. But behind US Steel's facade of benevolence lay a hard-edged commitment to maximizing shareholder returns and oppressing workers.

For example, the company took pride in building twenty-five thousand houses for staff, but the vast majority were reserved for higher-level employees. Only 5 percent of the workforce actually employed in steelmaking—ten thousand out of two hundred thousand steelworkers—had access to company housing.[17]

The company boasted it had a job safety record second to none, but it could have done far better. Workers pleaded for a reduction in the twelve-hour workday, as steel mills were dangerous places to work, and fatigue was a major cause of avoidable injuries and deaths on the job. When the company finally agreed to an eight-hour day in 1923, the number and severity of accidents fell substantially.

Even the company's two most lauded innovations—employee stock ownership and a company-funded pension plan—delivered much less than they promised. Employees purchasing shares paid for them in installments over three years, but turnover at some factories was over 50 percent per year, leading to a high rate of default on stock payments. Only about 15 percent of employees successfully participated in the program.

But that was an order of magnitude more than the number of employees who received pensions from the company, about 1.2 percent. This was not a surprising result given that the minimum retirement age was sixty-five and the required length of service was twenty-five years. Very few workers lasted that long in the crucible of the steel industry.

When softer measures failed to keep workers tractable, US Steel resorted readily to coercion. An extensive network of spies created anxiety and undercut job security. Any report of interest in organizing a union, or other "disloyal" sentiment, led to immediate dismissal and being named to a "blacklist" that made it impossible to find employment at other steel companies.

Management deliberately varied production as a tactic to let workers know their jobs should not be taken for granted, ramping up inventory then shutting down lines and laying off workers for indefinite periods, even when demand for products was stable. Only those deemed "loyal" were invited back to their jobs.

The combination of illusory benefits and ruthless oppression kept US Steel's factories free of union penetration for three decades.

In its mature phase, up until the Great Depression of the 1930s, welfare capitalism was a feature at about 80 percent of America's largest companies. Many workers saw through the hypocrisy. Data is scarce, but a number of anecdotal reports indicate that employees frequently asked companies to abandon paternalistic benefits in favor of better wages and shorter hours. For example, when employees were polled at one large company on their preference for job incentives, "welfare work" came last in the list of five, behind job security, remuneration, opportunity for promotion, and advancement by ability.[18]

Welfare capitalism came on the cheap, averaging about 2 percent of the payroll,[19] but paid off handsomely for those at the top. The richest 10 percent of Americans saw their share of total income rise in the 1920s from 38 to 47 percent,[20] while manufacturing wages declined[21] despite strong economic growth overall, and union membership sank from 17 percent of the workforce to 11 percent.[22]

4 The Power Triangle

The federal government exercised its newfound rights to oversee business in the public interest only tentatively, until the cataclysm of the Great Depression forced its hand.

The Depression had its origin in an unrestrained credit boom, similar to earlier financial crises. Aggressive lending in the 1920s inflated asset prices and spurred overinvestment in many sectors, especially real estate, consumer durables, and investments.[1] The stock market grew by 500 percent, ten times as fast as the gross domestic product (GDP), much of it fueled by borrowed money, leading to massive overvaluation.

When the stock market bubble finally burst in 1929, it sent shock waves throughout the economy. Anxious depositors demanded immediate liquidity, and banks that could not comply—about a third of the total—closed their doors. In a downward spiral, companies without credit lines cut production or went under, throwing workers off the payroll, which eroded demand for goods and services. Weak demand deflated prices, dramatically raising the real cost of money and further increasing the strain on business.

Franklin D. Roosevelt was elected to lead the shattered country in 1932 and promised a "New Deal" to stabilize the economy, restart growth, and provide a social safety net to protect individual and family well-being. Under FDR, who served as president until his death in 1945, the federal government expanded its remit in stunning fashion, aiding business but also imposing new obligations.

Companies, finally, were prohibited from hiring children. A minimum wage was put in place, and overtime was mandated for a workday exceeding eight hours. Among the most significant reforms, the role of labor unions was formally recognized for the first time. Workers gained legal protection against being fired for organizing or joining unions. Companies were required to bargain collectively with unions that had majority support within a workplace. Employers were banned from setting up "company unions" under their control.

Early in the New Deal, business leaders mounted a counteroffensive by forming the American Liberty League, which claimed 125,000 members, led by industrialists like General Motors President Alfred P. Sloan and the DuPont family, owners of the giant chemical company. Their strategy was to resurrect the fear of socialism, this time tagging it to the state rather than to organized labor.

The group tried to bolster its credibility by recruiting Al Smith, formerly a Progressive and the Democratic Party's candidate for president in 1928, as its spokesperson. In a nationwide radio broadcast in January 1936, Smith exhorted his listeners, "Get the platform of the Democratic Party and get the platform of the Socialist Party and lay them down on your dining-room table, side by side. . . . Pick up the platform that more nearly squares with the record, and you will have your hand on the Socialist platform."[2]

But even with an icon like Smith heading the charge, the accusation that the New Deal was socialism in disguise failed to gain traction with the public, and the League soon declined. Like the rest of the country, the business community seemed dazzled by the hectic experiments and bold initiatives that Roosevelt rolled out continuously during his tenure and were unable to form a coherent position.

The New Deal eased, but did not cure, the Depression—that would take the full employment and massive economic stimulus of World War II, which the United States joined in 1941. But during this period, the roles of business, labor unions, and government were becoming more clearly defined, gradually interlocking in a stable power triangle.

Each leg of the power triangle played a critical role in the quarter century of fast, broad-based economic growth that followed the end of the war in 1945. This period, 1948–1973, is often called the Golden Age of Capitalism. The economy almost tripled, with GDP growth of 4.1 percent per year outstripping both the rate in the 1930s, 1.3 percent, and in the years since the close of this period, 2.7 percent.[3]

Moreover, the gains from growth were more equitably shared than at any time before or since. Family income doubled for the bottom 20 percent.[4] The share of income for the top 10 percent came down to about 35 percent, compared to 47 percent in 1929. Their share of national wealth dropped to 65 percent from its peak of 80 percent in 1910.[5]

The state's responsibility for certain social obligations was now recognized as a core function, not just an emergency measure.[6] Government invested in infrastructure, like the interstate highway system, and continued to expand social programs, contributing one-quarter, 0.63 percent, to the total 2.5 percent average growth in GDP per capita.[7]

Corporations and rich individuals paid taxes at rates that seem high today but formed part of a political and social consensus. The top marginal income tax rate for companies was around 50 percent and for individuals about 80 percent, versus 21 percent and 41 percent, respectively, in 2024.

Labor unions were at their height, having grown rapidly during wartime, when industry accepted to cooperate with unions in exchange for a tacit no-strike pledge. Union membership rose from 2.8 million in 1933 to 14 million in 1945, about 36 percent of the workforce.

Unions raised wages both by their own success in negotiating on behalf of their members and the example they set for nonunion workplaces. Typically, union members benefit from a "union wage premium" of around 20 percent, and unionization leads to improved standards for benefits like retirement plans and medical care.[8]

Now that welfare was acknowledged as the obligation of the state, business leaders could finally put aside the flimflam of welfare capitalism, and business as a "public trust," and return to the dictum that making money is its own reward.

Dow Chemical Company President Leland J. Doan expressed the consensus with refreshing candor. He had an opinion piece published in 1957 with the headline "Fundamental Role of Business Is to Operate Profitably": "Any activity labeled 'social responsibility' must be judged in terms of whether it is somehow beneficial to the immediate or long-range welfare of the business. . . . Our first responsibility is profitable operation. . . . A second responsibility of management is protection of the owner's capital. . . . I hope we never kid ourselves that we are operating for the public interest per se."[9]

Doan was in good company. The president of mighty US Steel, Roger M. Blough, made it clear in 1963 that he also had no intention of "operating for the public interest."

Civil rights were growing into a burning issue across the country, and US Steel was being taken to task for racial segregation and discrimination, especially in its Southern operations. But Blough was obdurate. His meaning was clear, though his language was mannered: "For a corporation to attempt to exert any kind of economic compulsion to achieve a particular end in the social area seems to me to be quite beyond what a corporation should do."[10]

Prominent academic Andrew Hacker said the same thing but more clearly. Hacker, who later wrote a best-selling book on race in America, *Two Nations: Black and White, Separate, Hostile, Unequal*, gave Blough unequivocal support: "Preserving civil rights and civil liberties, and promoting internal security and the general welfare, are the tasks of judges, politicians, and the American people themselves. If corporations ought to be doing things they are not now doing—such as hiring Negroes on an equal basis with whites—then it is up to government to tell them so. The only responsibility of corporations is to make profits, thus contributing to a prosperous economic system."[11]

Blough and Hacker knew their constituency well. Although there were some exceptions, the corporate community overall did not make significant voluntary strides toward racial equality and only moved materially to end discrimination in the workplace when forced to do so by the landmark Civil Rights Act of 1964.[12]

Industry vigorously opposed environmental objectives as well as social ones, denying strong scientific evidence of the health hazards of air pollution and claiming the costs of reducing emissions would outweigh the benefits. "Just wishing for it won't make the air cleaner," admonished a booklet published by Mobil Oil Corp. (now part of ExxonMobil Corporation) in the 1960s. "It will cost a lot of money. And sooner or later the cost will fall on the people. All the people."[13]

Mobil was half right. The costs imposed by limiting emissions from smokestacks and tailpipes *are* sizable, about $65 billion per year, according to the Environmental Protection Agency (EPA). But Mobil was also totally wrong. The EPA estimates that the annual benefits, in terms of lives saved, health improved, and productivity enhanced, are thirty times greater than the cost: about $2 trillion.[14]

5 The New Gilded Age

The Golden Age of Capitalism drew to a close by 1973, when oil producers, led by Saudi Arabia, instigated a worldwide recession by imposing an oil embargo on the United States and some other Western countries to punish them for supporting Israel in a war with Egypt and Syria. Oil supplied almost half of America's total energy needs, and its sudden scarcity in an economy that was already slowing led to price hikes and disruptions, including long lines at gas stations that infuriated motorists.

Another oil shock landed in 1979 when Iran's revolution shut down much of its petroleum production. In less than a decade, oil prices had risen by six times. This gave strong impetus to cost-led inflation, accompanied by high unemployment—a disheartening phenomenon known as "stagflation" that government policy seemed helpless to stem. The dismal economic scene fed a wave of discontent that gave Ronald Reagan a decisive win in the 1980 presidential contest.

The rise of Reagan spelled the end of the national consensus around New Deal–style government interventionism. "Government is not the solution to our problem," he famously declared. "Government is the problem." The power triangle was set for dismantling.

Reagan's chief economic advisor, Milton Friedman, a Nobel Prize–winning libertarian economist, lent academic credibility to policies designed to expand the power of business. Already in 1970 he had captured the zeitgeist of the corporate community, declaring, "There is one and only one social responsibility of business—to use its resources and engage in activities designed to increase its profits."[1] This paean to shareholder value is still widely cited today.

Reagan was quick to act, spearheading a drive for lower corporate tax rates in his first administration that allowed half of America's 250 largest corporations to pay no income tax, despite substantial profitability. Overall, corporate income tax fell as a share of federal government revenue from 25 percent in the 1950s and 1960s to 6 percent by 1983.[2] Reagan and his allies deregulated the banking and natural gas industries, lifted price controls on airfares, eased air pollution controls, and opened up vast amounts of government-owned land to oil drilling and other private development.

Perhaps Reagan's most consequential pro-business move was to vitiate anti-monopoly enforcement, on the principle that businesses that dominate their sector are doing nothing wrong unless output shrinks or prices increase.[3] As the government watchdog slept, companies began buying each other at rates not seen since the formation of the competition-killing corporate trusts around the turn of the century. With Reagan in the White House, the Department of Justice (DOJ) only filed two anti-monopoly cases versus fifty-two in the prior decade.[4]

While Reagan pampered business, he pummeled organized labor. Reagan's appointees to the National Labor Relations Board, charged with enforcing laws to protect union activity, were uniformly pro-management and anti-union in their judgments.[5] Reagan encouraged employer recalcitrance and intimidated labor unions when, early in his administration, he fired eleven thousand striking air traffic controllers.

Minimizing government called for unraveling the social safety net. To fund tax cuts, Reagan rolled back welfare programs, ending aid to more than four hundred thousand families with dependent children and tightening food stamp eligibility to exclude one million people who would have qualified previously. Spending on programs for low-income recipients under Reagan was about 29 percent less than it would have been absent his changes.[6]

The Reagan-era policies of freer markets, smaller government, fewer social services, lower taxes, less business regulation, lax labor law enforcement, and more open international trade are known collectively as "neoliberalism." With the exception of foreign trade, which has lost much of its allure for both right and left, neoliberalism is still the reigning paradigm in the United States.

By the end of the Reagan era, after only a few years of neoliberalism ascendancy, the trend toward greater income equality had reversed. The income of the top 10 percent of earners had risen from 35 percent of the total when Reagan took office to 40 percent.[7] And in the four decades since Reagan set the new mold, corporate power has continued to rise, while workers have gone backward and income inequality has deepened.

Union membership has shrunk from 24 percent at the advent of the Reagan era to 10 percent.[8] With union strength ebbing, wages have stagnated. In the Golden Age of Capitalism, average wages rose in lockstep with productivity, 91 percent and 97 percent, respectively. By contrast, although productivity rose a further 74 percent in the following four decades, 1973–2013, wages only rose 9 percent in real terms.[9]

For those at the bottom of the pay scale, compensation has actually fallen in real terms by 5 percent.[10] This is not surprising in light of the fact that the minimum wage has shrunk by 40 percent, in inflation-adjusted dollars, from its peak value in 1968.[11]

Instead of productivity benefits going to workers, they have fattened corporate bottom lines, with after-tax profit margins averaging 9 percent since 2010—50 percent higher than during the Golden Age.[12]

In the absence of government oversight, corporations have once again used their great wealth to combine into domineering behemoths. Completed mergers skyrocketed by a factor of seven in 1985–2017, from 2,308 annually to 15,361.[13]

In the thirty years after Reagan left the White House, the DOJ filed only ten anti-monopoly cases. Civil suits by the DOJ's antitrust division for non-merger issues also fell dramatically.[14] The administration of Joe Biden in 2021–2024 was more active in antitrust than any presidency since Reagan's, but it could not undo in four years the buildup of corporate concentration that had mounted unimpeded during the previous forty. And when Donald Trump took power for the second time in 2025, the pendulum swung back to quiescent antitrust enforcement.

As a result of decades of government inaction, over 75 percent of US industries have become more concentrated since the 1990s.[15] With competition sidelined, corporate giants are free to hike prices, stifle innovation, and erode worker rights.

CEOs have been richly rewarded for suppressing wages and easing competition. Their average pay has risen to around 350 times the compensation of the average worker, from a ratio of 23 times in 1973.[16]

Mark Twain would feel at home in today's America, though he would skewer the excesses of our own Gilded Age as relentlessly as he did his own.

The richest 10 percent of Americans now own about as high a proportion of the country's wealth as they did in Twain's time, around 67 percent.[17] Their share of national income, above 45 percent, is *higher* than during the Gilded Age.[18] Meanwhile, the bottom half of the population only owns about 3 percent of national wealth,[19] *much less* than their relative share of 12 percent in 1890.

America's GINI score, an overall measure of income inequality, is on a par with the highest level it has ever registered, in 1874.[20]

As in the days of Progressivism, corporate leaders often use public-minded rhetoric to shield an unremitting commitment to shareholder primacy. The most notable recent example is the issuance of a new definition of the "Purpose of a Corporation" in 2019 by the Business Roundtable, America's most elite and influential business group, made up of CEOs of the country's largest corporations.[21]

Introducing the statement, Jamie Dimon—chairman and CEO of the nation's largest bank, JPMorgan Chase, and chair of Business Roundtable—warned, "The American dream is alive, but fraying. Major employers are investing in their workers and communities because they know it is the only way to be successful over the long term. These modernized principles reflect the business community's unwavering commitment to continue to push for an economy that serves all Americans."

Knowingly or not, Dimon was invoking the ghost of George Perkins, the progenitor of US Steel's exploitative welfare capitalism: "The larger the corporation becomes, the greater become its responsibilities to the entire community. The corporations of the future must be those that are semi-public servants."[22]

The Roundtable said its new policy "moves away from shareholder primacy [and] includes [a] commitment to all stakeholders." It went on:

> We commit to: Delivering value to our customers. . . . Investing in our employees. This starts with compensating them fairly and providing important benefits. . . . Dealing fairly and ethically with our suppliers. . . . Supporting the communities in which we work. We respect the people in our communities and protect the environment. . . . Each of our stakeholders is essential. We commit to deliver value to all of them, for the future success of our companies, our communities and our country.

The statement drew wide praise and was taken as the corporate community's definitive embrace of socially positive behavior. But companies that signed the pledge failed to honor their commitments.

Two years after the Roundtable published its groundbreaking declaration, a study compared the performance of the companies that signed the statement to those that did not. It found that pledge takers performed worse, not better, than their peers in supporting stakeholders. They had more environmental- and labor-related compliance violations, higher carbon emissions, and a greater level of opposition to social resolutions proposed by shareholders, and they spent more on lobbying lawmakers for favorable legislation.

But they did outperform in one aspect: They had higher ESG scores.[23]

6 Understanding Corporate Amorality

In the face of mounting public evidence that smoking causes cancer, cigarette company CEOs met secretly in December 1953 and decided to counterattack: to create a research institute under their control with the sole mission of casting doubt on independent data—to use science against science.

In an era when science was held in high regard and assumed to be directed for the benefit of the public, this innovative tactic was brilliant—and turned out to be highly successful. For more than three decades, a flood of biased studies from the tobacco research organization created false doubt in the minds of Americans and helped sustain cigarette consumption per capita in the United States at or above 1950 levels, despite overwhelming evidence of its harm. Millions died needlessly.

Within the tobacco industry itself, there was little doubt. A chemist at R. J. Reynolds, maker of popular brands like Lucky Strike and Camel, conducted a comprehensive survey of the literature in 1953, reviewing seventy-eight scientific papers. It concluded, in careful but clear language, that "studies of clinical data tend to confirm the relationship between heavy and prolonged tobacco smoking and incidence of cancer of the lung." Furthermore, extensive testing of tobacco on animals "indicates the probable presence of carcinogenic agents in those substances."[1]

By 1961, the insiders at cigarette companies felt no need to pull punches. A memorandum from Ligget & Myers, maker of cigarette standards like L&M and Chesterfield, stated bluntly that there are "biologically active materials present in cigarette tobacco. These are: a) cancer-causing; b) cancer promoting; and c) poisonous."[2]

In the public sphere as well, evidence against smoking was mounting. In 1964, a blockbuster report by the Surgeon General should have cleared away any remaining question marks. The report found that an average smoker had a risk of developing lung cancer nine to ten times higher than nonsmokers. For heavy smokers, the increase was twenty times. Overall, smoking was responsible for a 70 percent higher mortality rate in smokers versus nonsmokers.[3]

A wave of alarm in the wake of the report persuaded Congress to require a health warning on all cigarette packages the next year. In 1969, cigarette advertising was banned on television and radio.

By 1970, cigarette per capita consumption had crested, finally, and was ebbing, yet it was still 13 percent *higher* than in 1950.[4] During this period, the cigarette industry had managed, through its own misleading studies, to completely neutralize the effect on public opinion of the massive amount of independent research showing that smoking causes cancer.

Big Tobacco's successful weapon against science was known as the Tobacco Industry Research Committee (TIRC), founded in 1953 after the cigarette company CEOs, during their secret summit, approved a proposal for its creation from John W. Hill, founder of the public relations firm Hill & Knowlton.

Hill's company set up and firmly controlled the institute, to the point of sharing an office with it and choosing one of its own executives, W. T. Hoyt, who had no scientific experience, to lead it. Hill's firm selected all the members of the Scientific Advisory Board, which reviewed grant proposals from the institute's staff.

The genius of the TIRC was performing research into the causes of cancer that appeared meaningful but was completely irrelevant, as it pointed in all directions *except* tobacco. The TIRC's first scientific director, Clarence Cook Little, listed its subject areas in 1959: heredity, infection, nutrition, hormones, nervous strain or tension, and environmental factors.[5] None of them held a candle to smoking as a determinant of lung cancer. In 1960, Little explained in court that the TIRC was not conducting studies on tobacco smoke because it had never proven to be cancerous, a self-fulfilling proposition that the TIRC, later renamed the Council for Tobacco Research, held steadfastly during its forty-five-year history.[6]

The tobacco industry cited the research it had commissioned as if it were independent, using it to champion the claim that smoking could not be singled out as a cause of cancer. As Philip Morris, maker of the best-selling brand Marlboro, said in a publication entitled "Facts About the Smoking

Controversy" in 1978, "Scientists have not determined what causes cancer . . . Cigarettes have not been proven unsafe."[7]

Big Tobacco wielded this pretense of doubt to fend off regulation of the cigarette industry, and as a defense against lawsuits that were beginning to pile up from cancer-stricken smokers. But the main purpose of the biased research was to blow smoke into the public's eyes so that nicotine addicts would not be motivated to kick the habit, and new recruits would fall into it.

The ploy worked better than the cigarette executives could have imagined. In 1970, six years after the Surgeon General's damning report, when smokers were asked if the statement "Cigarette smoking in moderation is safe" is true or not, 68 percent responded "true" or "don't know." A quarter century after that, 60 percent of smokers *still* did not believe that they were at a higher risk of cancer.[8]

Smoking might still be aswirl in uncertainty were it not for a massive legal settlement between cigarette companies and forty-six states in 1998 that required the dissolution of the tobacco industry's captive research arm and the payment of more than $200 billion to states to fund anti-smoking campaigns as well as medical care for tobacco-related illnesses. Without Big Tobacco stoking the fire of doubt, the understanding that smoking kills has gradually permeated the public consciousness.

The pernicious precedent that tobacco set—undermining the credibility of science in order to advance self-interest—has become a standard tactic of corporations and partisan interest groups. Just a few years after the tobacco industry broke the path, the sugar industry followed in its footsteps, sponsoring questionable research that downplayed the role of sucrose in heart disease.[9] Other food industries have followed its lead. A review in 2007 of more than two hundred studies of the health effects of eating certain foods found that when food companies sponsored the research, it was four to eight times more likely to come up with positive findings.[10]

Climate change has also been targeted. The fossil fuel industry hid explosive research evidence for years in a successful bid to stall effective climate action. Scientists at Exxon Corporation (now ExxonMobil Corporation) in the 1970s and '80s were uncannily prescient and precise in their predictions of global warming from fossil fuels. But company executives suppressed the research internally and rejected its implications publicly. Said CEO Lee Raymond in 1999, "[climate] projections are based on completely unproven climate models, or, more often, sheer speculation."[11]

We can accept some corner cutting as "business as usual" in a competitive market. But when corporate amorality attains deadly levels—like cigarette makers who kill their customers and oil companies who close their eyes to climate disaster—it becomes important to ask ourselves how people who presumably have positive personal moral values can willingly abandon them when managing businesses.

Thinking like the Group

We can begin to understand this phenomenon by referring to a *New York Times Magazine* article from 1994 by Roger Rosenblatt. The author interviewed a number of Philip Morris senior executives, four years before the Tobacco Master Settlement Agreement forced the industry to admit explicitly that cigarettes are harmful.[12] By that point, the industry's strategy had moved from overtly rejecting claims of harm to insisting on people's right to assess risks for themselves and make choices.

The company's general counsel, Steve Parrish, a smoker, told Rosenblatt that he felt bad for Rose Cipollone, whose civil suit against Philip Morris and other cigarette manufacturers for causing her cancer was covered extensively in the national press. (She was awarded $400,000, but the judgment was overturned on appeal.) He described Rose as "a really neat lady," adding, "I met her a couple of times before she died. She was sort of spunky, you know. And Mr. Cipollone was a very nice man. . . . But I really did feel strongly that he was not entitled to get money because his wife chose to smoke."

Personal liberty was also the key to smoking's defense for David Dangoor, the company's executive vice president for international operations, also a smoker: "I'm sure that people think smoking is even more dangerous than it ever could be. Yet they do it. Why? Is it an addiction issue? I don't believe it. People do all sorts of things to express their individuality and to protest against society. And smoking is one of them, and not the worst."

Overall, Rosenblatt found the senior managers to be "intelligent and companionable; most are family-oriented and community minded. . . . All are well paid, but not much more than executives at other large companies." And here are key points: "All feel beleaguered by portions of society . . . and by the news media and the 'antis,' whom they alternately call 'Nazis' or 'smoking police'. . . . Every one of them expresses enormous affection and respect for the company."

Listen to Steve Parrish on why he joined the company after being an outside lawyer: "Philip Morris is a great company in terms of its business success, its reputation and all that sort of thing. The people really impressed me. And I really like representing the tobacco workers, who run the machinery and make the cigarettes. Really good people—the kind I thought I'd represent when I was growing up."

Or consider David Dangoor, reflecting on almost two decades of service with the company: "I must tell you, the people you have around you every day, and the kind of environment that you live in every day, become an incredibly important part of the quality of your life. The issues that you refer to [i.e., harm from smoking] become less important, not because you deny the problems but because as a whole it's not the question of making more money. It's the question of being very happy at doing what you're doing."

Without knowing it, the Philip Morris executives were presenting a textbook example of the psychological phenomenon known as "groupthink," a term coined in 1952 by *Fortune* magazine writer William Whyte,[13] then systematized as a condition by Yale psychologist Irving Janis in 1971.[14] Whyte was writing about conformism in a postwar world, where (mostly) men had transitioned, usually smoothly, from the chain of command of the military to the hierarchy of business. (He went on to write a seminal book on mid-century corporate culture, *The Organization Man*, which is still cited today.)

Almost two decades later, Janis set forth a general theory of groupthink, incorporating Whyte's views and others into his own thirty years of research into group dynamics. His main principle was that "the more amiability and esprit de corps there is among the members of a policy-making ingroup, the greater the danger that independent critical thinking will be replaced by groupthink, which is likely to result in irrational and dehumanizing actions directed against outgroups."

A "key characteristic" of groupthink, said Janis, is "remaining loyal to the group by sticking with the policies to which the group has already committed itself, even when those policies are obviously working out badly and have unintended consequences that disturb the conscience of each member." Stress heightens in-group loyalty, he found.

Janis cited the example of Arthur Schlesinger Jr., a special assistant to President John F. Kennedy. Schlesinger was ardently opposed to the United States backing Cuban exiles in an invasion to overthrow Fidel

Castro—rightly so, as the Bay of Pigs invasion in 1961 turned out to be a fiasco, strengthening Castro's hold on power and inflicting lasting damage on US foreign policy.

In the run-up to the disaster, Schlesinger made his views known in private memos to the president but stayed quiet during the meetings of senior leaders in which agreement was eventually reached to undertake the project. Later, he said, "I bitterly reproached myself for having kept so silent during those crucial discussions. . . . One's impulse to blow the whistle on this nonsense was simply undone by the circumstances of the discussion."

The hypnotic nature of groupthink can seem contrived to someone who has not experienced it. So let me tell you a personal story.

Many years ago, I was a junior diplomat in an American embassy in a small African country that had recently experienced a bloody coup d'état and was being run by a group of thuggish, low-ranking soldiers. My employer, the State Department, took the view that we could contain the worst practices of the coup leaders, stabilize the country, and persuade the military rulers to hold democratic elections, peacefully handing power over to civilians. This ambitious policy was put into motion, using large amounts of foreign aid and intensive diplomacy.

Part of my job was to analyze political views among the host country population. In the absence of political parties and a free press, I established an informal network of sources, a number of whom also became social contacts. They were unanimous in assessing that the country's rulers were thoroughly corrupt and brutal and would never agree to free and fair elections. From my own observations and perceptions, I had to agree. I spoke up for this perspective in internal discussions at the embassy for a while, but my voice carried little weight, and over time I quieted down.

As the timeline for the democratic transition grew shorter, my responsibilities grew. The embassy instigated the naming of independent commissions to draft a new constitution and organize elections. This was uncharted territory for the country, and I spent many days helping the newly appointed election officials cope with complex issues around the creation of democratic institutions. I also pushed hard within the US government for grant funding to ensure that the machinery for elections kept rolling forward. I reported diligently on each bit of incremental progress and received compliments for my work and analysis, both within the embassy and from headquarters in Washington, DC.

The embassy was a close-knit community of dedicated diplomats, with a clearly defined mission, and I was proud to be a member of the team. I admired my colleagues and felt valued and respected. Gradually, I let the presumption that my assignment was correct filter into the normative part of my thinking and take precedence over my visceral doubt about the credibility of our objective. I tuned out the dissident voices of my friends in the local community, who never wavered in their conviction that America was building an elaborate sand castle that would crumble instantly when put to the test. No longer a reluctant facilitator of the policy, I became its sincere advocate.

I thought like the group.

I left for a tour of duty in Washington some months before the scheduled elections in the country. Out of the hothouse of the embassy, I began to regain a more balanced viewpoint. I felt acute discomfort when the State Department gave me a medal for my efforts to help prepare the ground for a democratic transformation in the country. I began to doubt whether I belonged in the Foreign Service at all and resigned two years later.

The coda to the story: My local friends were dead right. Rather than stepping down, as we had hoped, the head of the military junta ran for president and blatantly falsified the election results to claim victory. His misrule grew ever more autocratic and erratic, leading a few years later to a complete breakdown of order, followed by a multiyear period of civil conflict marked by extreme violence and massive destruction.

Whether you believe that groupthink can be validly isolated as a distinct psychological phenomenon or not, and some psychologists do not,[15] it is clear that people bring traits like loyalty, group cohesion, and disagreement aversion to decision-making. In the focused world of corporate leadership, under stress to achieve challenging financial targets, often in the face of powerful competitors, it is not hard to understand how participants arrive at an implicit consensus to suspend personal value judgments.

The implication is not that business leaders are immoral or that procedures must be, or even can be, implemented to impede the development of groupthink within executive suites. It is that corporations by their nature are morally blind, and that constraints on their behavior arise not from not the ethical or moral principles of their leaders but from market forces and legal constraints.

This understanding helps us interpret and put in context the misleading investment strategies and greenwashing of socially responsible finance.

To sum up, here is the acute but sad perspective of a tobacco industry insider who talked to Rosenblatt as he was dying of lung cancer and trying to come to grips with the irony. Said Victor L. Crawford, a former Maryland state senator who served as a senior lobbyist for the tobacco industry and was instrumental in defeating several anti-smoking bills,

> I've got nobody to blame but myself. I knew what it was. But the tobacco companies were culpable, too. I had some twinges when I was lobbying for them. Why don't they have a feeling of responsibility?. . . . These hard-nosed tobacco execs say that they have a perfect right to do what they do. But they must know. They have to know. Because they're brilliant people. And they're tough, hard businessmen. They know. But they're able to sublimate it. . . . "Freedom of choice is more important than anything!" Well, that's not necessarily true. But it offers a way that you can live with yourself. . . . In my heart, I knew better. But I rationalized and denied, because the money was so good and because I could always rationalize it. That's how you make a living, by rationalizing that black is not black; it's white, it's green, it's yellow. But I knew, in my heart, that what the Surgeon General said was right. I think these people know that.

II The Myth of Doing Well by Doing Good

7 Denying the Social-Financial Trade-Off

Before the term "ESG" was coined, socially responsible investment had been practiced for almost eighty years. But it had been a backwater of the finance industry, appealing to investors who wanted to shun objectionable companies, even if that meant lower investment returns.

The first SRI fund, the Pioneer Fund, opened its doors in 1928, shortly after the establishment of mutual funds began to draw retail investors into the stock market. Mutual funds appealed to individuals and families by providing exposure to a wide swath of shares for a relatively small capital commitment.

Funds soon began to offer distinct investment strategies to compete for investor dollars. The Pioneer Fund, many of whose initial investors were religious, was the first to adopt the policy of banishing alcohol and cigarettes from its portfolio. This practice of excluding stocks on ethical grounds was soon imitated by other fund managers and targeted to general investor audiences. The strategy became known as "negative screening."

At first, the targets for screening were the "sin" industries alcohol, gambling, and tobacco, traditionally referred to as "booze, bets, and butts." As sustainable investing developed, other controversial sectors were added to the list, such as weapons manufacturers, nuclear power, and fossil fuels, with each fund choosing its own mix of disfavored sectors to avoid.

Negative screening may help investors feel more in tune with their moral codes, but it typically has no effect on the stock prices of excluded companies and thus no effect on their social behavior.

When you buy or sell a share on the stock market, your counterpart is another investor, not the company directly, except in the relatively rare case of the company offering new stock to the public. The volume of trading due to new stock issues—called "primary" share offerings—is minuscule compared to the buy and sell action in previously issued stock, called "secondary" shares.

Since you are almost always dealing in secondary shares, your trades have no direct effect on the finances of the companies whose stocks you trade, only the gains or losses of the investors you deal with. In principle, if enough investors sell in concert, a stock's price will be pushed down, which would raise the company's cost of capital. But in practice, capital markets for listed companies are so large that negative screening has no discernible effect on their price levels (as we discuss in chapter 11).

Screening does not push companies forward socially, but it does push investors back financially. Excluding stocks from a portfolio breaks the first law of asset management: diversify. Diversification reduces the price volatility of a portfolio of stocks because it dilutes the effects of price movements of individual stocks. Many sin sectors are relatively large, so barring a number of them lowers diversification significantly and raises volatility.

In addition, many sin companies, like cigarette makers and oil majors, typically have high profit margins and robust stock price performance, so excluding them heightens the probability of lower returns overall, compared to a broad market fund.

The empirical evidence is not unanimous, but a strong consensus exists among researchers that negative screening exacts a price. As a comprehensive paper sums up, "Investing in controversial stocks in many cases results in additional risk-adjusted returns, whereas excluding them may reduce financial performance."[1]

A simple rule applies to investment strategy: If you want market returns, buy the market.

Financial institutions, which hold about 80 percent of total stock market capitalization,[2] feel this tension as acutely as retail investors, as they are judged by how well they make decisions on behalf of those whose money they manage. Financial managers are typically fiduciaries, meaning they have a legal obligation to act in the best interests of their clients, usually interpreted as striving for the best financial returns possible. But their customers want asset managers to be good citizens as well as earn market-rate financial returns. Asset managers and institutions are caught in a dilemma: eager to show socially responsible credentials but not free to put investment returns at risk.

Interest in SRI was muted for the first few decades after its founding but ramped up in the 1960s, a time of dramatic social and political change. As opposition to the Vietnam War built, anti-war protesters called for divestment from companies that supplied the military, like Dow Chemical Company (now Dow, Inc.), whose napalm product causes horrific burns and was used by the Pentagon in Vietnam as an anti-personnel weapon. Concurrently, the civil rights movement turned a spotlight on corporate racial discrimination.

In the 1970s, environmental degradation came to the forefront of public concern, leading to the enactment of landmark laws to limit industrial emissions, like the Clean Air Act and the Clean Water Act, and the establishment of the EPA. Investors and the public began demanding that corporations be held accountable for their role in pollution.

In the 1980s, revulsion over the segregationist policies of South Africa led to a global campaign to divest from South African stocks and boycott South African companies and those doing business with the apartheid regime. This also led to heightened scrutiny of companies' human rights performance in other countries as well.

In the 1990s, dawning recognition of climate warming and the role of corporations in the climate crisis redoubled the commitment of retail investors to force companies into assuming greater social responsibility.

A tide of capital with social intentions was rising, seeking an outlet. But traditional methods, focusing on negative screening, were unable to channel this flow, as their inability to provide assurances of market-rate financial returns limited their audience.

The floodgates opened in 2004 with the introduction of the term ESG to the financial industry via a report, *Who Cares Wins*, authored by twenty large international financial institutions under the sponsorship of the United Nations.[3] (Inexplicably, the title is a pun on the motto of the United Kingdom's Special Air Service, a covert, anti-terrorist military force: "Who Dares Wins.")

The report noted that nontraditional risks—"emerging environmental and social trends, in combination with rising public expectations for better accountability and corporate governance"—were rising in importance and deserved more attention from investment analysts, money managers, and company CEOs.

Who Cares Wins highlighted three areas of concern:

- *Environmental* issues included coping with the operational and financial stress of climate change and anticipating more stringent regulation on emissions.
- *Social* issues included workplace health and safety, community relations, and human rights issues.
- Corporate *governance* matters included independent members on the board of directors and "linking executive compensation to longer-term drivers of shareholder value."

The report's key contention was that effectively managing these risks would improve company financial performance. It quoted the chief investment officer of the largest pension fund in the Netherlands: "There is a growing body of empirical evidence that companies which manage environmental, social and governance risks most effectively tend to deliver better risk-adjusted financial performance than their industry peers."

But if such evidence existed, *Who Cares Wins* did not provide it. The report was heavy on rhetoric but light on proof. It only presented two studies with any specificity. Both dealt with relevant industries for environmental concerns—fossil fuels and the automotive industry—but their findings undermined rather than strengthened the purported link between ESG and profitability.

The mission of the first study highlighted in *Who Cares Wins* was to quantify "to the extent possible" the impact of environmental and social issues on the stock prices of major fossil fuel companies. But unfortunately, the report found, the extent possible was zero.[4]

"A strong performance in social and environmental issues is no guarantee of stock market performance," the report concluded. It added, "One-off environmental and social issues have limited impact on share prices unless they have a material impact on the underlying returns of the company in question." But this is just stating the obvious. Of course, the financial returns of a company typically affect the stock price.

However, the study did succeed in finding one material connection between social value and shareholder value: Companies that earned the researchers' highest social ranking also had the largest share of new production projects, a promising sign of future profits. But common sense says that is backward. The most socially positive oil companies should be *least* active in new projects, turning their efforts toward creating a future without oil instead of ceaselessly drilling for more. Awarding the highest social scores to the largest producers casts serious doubt on the credibility of the entire social ranking methodology.

The second study, on the automotive industry, also reported findings that appeared to confirm its hypothesis but fell apart upon closer examination. It concluded that climate change policies are very important, as they would have material effects on the projected net income of ten major car makers. But the effects were not all in the same direction. In fact, the study estimated that earnings would go up for half of the car companies and down for the other half—netting out to about zero overall.[5]

Using this data, an astute investor could neutralize the impact of climate change policies by investing equally across all ten companies. The more earnings sank for some, the more they would rise for others. This balanced investment strategy would lead to the same result as if climate change policies had *no* effect on car company earnings.

Despite its weak case, *Who Cares Wins* contained a kernel of truth. The growing importance of climate and social issues to a company's earnings should be recognized by executives, analysts, and investors. But recognizing risk is not the same as being able to capitalize on it for greater profitability.

"Soft" and "Hard" ESG

Despite the structural flaws in the argument of *Who Cares Wins*, the report primed the explosive growth of a new investment strategy. The prominence of its authors and sponsor lent the paper authority. But mostly, *Who Cares Wins* owed its success to providing investors, for the first time, with a promise of coupling social and financial returns that seemed genuine.

As a consequence, ESG has become a colossus. In the United States alone, $8.4 trillion is managed according to ESG principles, equivalent to about $25,000 for every person living in America. This is about 13 percent of the all the money under management in the country.[6] Worldwide, at $30 trillion, ESG accounts for an even greater proportion of assets under management, about one-quarter.[7]

If you have a retirement account, like a 401(k), some of your retirement savings may be in ESG funds. You may even have invested directly in one of the more than six hundred listed ESG funds in the United States that collectively manage about $1.2 trillion.[8]

An elaborate ecosystem has grown up around ESG—fund managers, rating agencies, analysts, consultants, advisors, marketers, and so forth. But the public this community serves doesn't understand the product.

To most people, ESG connotes a vague sense of positive corporate social behavior. A Gallup poll describes ESG as "includ[ing] factors like the record of a business on human rights, the environment, diversity or other social values" and finds that a majority of Americans, 60 percent, are familiar with it.[9] This is what I call "soft ESG"—more in tune with ethics than profits.

But the asset managers who invest ESG dollars, and the rating agencies whose scores guide those investments, understand ESG quite differently. They deal in what I call "hard ESG"—a quantitative measure of a company's ability to manage social and environmental risks that are financially material. Hard ESG is about investment decisions based on risk management for better financial performance—even if it leads to worse consequences for stakeholders other than shareholders.

The largest ESG asset manager in the world, BlackRock, explains that "environmental, social and governance (ESG) integration is the practice of incorporating ESG information into investment decisions to help enhance risk-adjusted returns."[10] Note what it does not say: that ESG aims to improve companies' social performance or make the world better.

Sustainalytics, a major ESG rating agency, owned by the prominent investment research firm Morningstar, Inc., assigns ESG ratings based on "a set of ESG-related factors that pose potential economic risks for companies."[11] No economic risk? No consideration.

A ratings handbook from another leading rating agency, MSCI, provides a deeper understanding of how ESG works in practice:

> MSCI ESG Ratings aim to measure a company's resilience to long-term, financially relevant ESG risks. . . . A risk is material to an industry when it is likely that companies in a given industry will incur substantial costs in connection with it (for example: regulatory ban on a key chemical input requiring reformulation). An opportunity is material to an industry when it is likely that companies in a given industry could capitalize on it for profit (for example: opportunities in clean technology for the LED lighting industry). The MSCI ESG Ratings model focuses *only on issues that are determined as material* for each.[12]

The text implies that an ESG risk (say, emitting tons of CO_2) is not material if it does not incur a cost to the company, and neither is an opportunity (say, increasing workforce diversity) material if it does not promise a profit. This would be deeply disturbing to anyone who thought ESG was about social value, regardless of financial impact.[13]

This reasoning explains why stocks in companies like cigarette makers turn up in ESG funds.

Philip Morris International Inc., maker of Marlboro, the most popular brand in America, boasts an ESG risk score of 21.2 from Sustainalytics, a "medium" level in its inverted scale ranging from 0, the best score, to 100. For its part, MSCI awards Philip Morris points for increasing the use of clean energy in its factories—not because decarbonization is good for the planet but because this makes the company better able to manage the risk to its bottom line of potential problems like rising oil and gas prices or regulatory limitations.[14]

Growing tobacco requires plentiful water, and MSCI praises Philip Morris for dealing well with "water stress." The "stress" MSCI is talking about refers not to the needs of the surrounding community for water but whether the cigarette manufacturer and its suppliers can get enough *for themselves* on terms they can afford.[15]

Tobacco companies' ESG ratings are high enough to give ESG funds cover to invest in them. For example, the Victory Sustainable World Fund, with $1.4 billion under management, has invested in Imperial Brands, formerly Imperial Tobacco, the world's fourth largest tobacco company. This fits well with its investment strategy: "incorporating financially material ESG considerations into the investment process in order to seek better risk-adjusted returns."[16]

Fossil fuel companies also get ESG scores in the average range despite spewing millions of tons of CO_2 into the air. Rating agency ISS-ESG, for example, gives three of the seven oil majors a C, two others a C+, and one (Eni) a B–.

ESG raters applaud the oil companies' risk management in areas such as health and safety, community relations, and waste management. The elephant in the room—their carbon emissions—doesn't count for much in the ratings, as oil is not going to be banned any time soon.

Given the rating agencies' blessing, ESG funds welcome Big Oil into their portfolios. The percentage of ESG funds that invest in fossil fuels, 83 percent, is just 1 percent less than mainstream funds that make no claim to be sustainable.[17]

There's a name for the social costs that are invisible to ESG: "negative externality." In economics, a negative externality is a cost that is inflicted by a force outside the control of the cost bearer. Healthcare expenses and lives lost from smoking are negative externalities, as the harm that arises from the actions of cigarette makers is borne by communities and families instead of the tobacco companies. In a similar manner, fossil fuel companies don't incur the costs of climate change—severe weather, flooding, wildfires, drought, excessive heat, and so on—brought about by using their products.

Corporate-caused negative externalities also include social problems such as poor nutrition and damaged health from junk foods, lives ruined and families broken by alcoholism, and financial ruin from gambling addiction. But sustainable investors are lulled by the high ESG scores of companies like Coca-Cola (MSCI rating: AAA), Diageo (AAA), and Flutter Entertainment (AA), awarded without taking negative externalities into account.

A true measurement of corporate social responsibility would be holistic, counting both the internal and external costs of a company's social risks. The results of such an analysis might lead sustainable funds to exclude fossil fuels completely, as well as some other sectors whose negative externalities outweigh their social good.

But this would be negative screening, to which ESG is supposed to be superior.

Many ESG funds try to have their cake and eat it too, by incorporating some negative screening, being careful not to overload the scale to reduce diversification materially and erode financial returns. But their main pitch is that good management of financially material social risks is good for business (even if not for society as a whole)—a claim, as we are about to see, that does not hold up under scrutiny.

8 Can Corporate Social Responsibility Be Monetized?

The best judges of ESG's effects on company profitability are the corporate executives who deal with it every day. In a survey of over five hundred corporate leaders, 60 percent said that a corporate ESG program was "very important." But when pushed to name ESG's biggest contribution to their financial performance, almost half the respondents, 48 percent, put "brand reputation" at the top. Less than one-third, 31 percent, said that ESG's biggest value was improving gross profits. Only 20 percent cited sales lead generation.[1]

The interpretation is clear: Senior managers think ESG is more important in public relations than in the actual operation of the company.

Fund managers agree on ESG's financial weakness. A survey of over five hundred fund managers ranked environmental and social (E&S) performance last in a list of six drivers of long-term value, behind such factors as strategy, competitive position, and capital structure. Even the ESG fund managers, who were half the number, sided with the others in placing E&S performance at the bottom of the pile.[2]

Although surveys provide useful insights, only empirical data can provide proof. Fortunately, thousands of research papers have tested for links between corporate social responsibility and financial strength. However, to get to the wheat, we have to separate it from the chaff.

If you did a Google search, you might quickly conclude that ESG leads to shareholder value as surely as dawn leads to day. The internet is full of ESG-positive studies that look like serious research to the lay reader but are more marketing than science. And search engines push these "infomercials" to the top of search results, while academic research falls to the bottom, languishing in specialist journals read only by experts.

For example, the accounting firm Moore Global has sponsored and published on their website a sensational report claiming that companies following ESG principles could *double* their rates of revenue and net income compared to others that were not ESG oriented.[3]

If all large companies in the covered region—the United States, Western Europe, and Australia—had pursued ESG policies in the three years previous to the report, their combined revenue increase would have been $4 trillion, the study estimated. Hence the eye-catching title of the report, "The $4 Trillion ESG Dividend."

But there are red flags all over the report. The first is that all we have to go on is an eleven-page, high-level, selective summary of a survey of more than one thousand companies. I asked for more detail from both Moore Global and the company they had commissioned to do the survey, but each politely declined. Research that is responsible usually contains detailed methodology and data so others can look critically at the evidence.

The key observation of the report was that revenue and profits had shot up among ESG "adopters," 10 percent and 9.1 percent, respectively, far exceeding ESG "laggards," whose comparable increases were 4.5 percent and 3.7 percent. In addition, 83 percent of the ESG leaders had increased customer retention, 86 percent had improved their brand image, and 84 percent believed they were more attractive to external investment.

The numbers are impressive, but the hazard flags are flying. Here are a few:

- *Confirmation bias:* Were the questions in the survey neutrally worded, or were they designed to elicit the positive responses that the authors may have been seeking? Without seeing the language, we cannot know.
- *Sample bias:* How were the survey respondents selected? Were they representative of the corporate community as a whole? Or was the sample stacked in favor of companies that found positive value in ESG?
- *Data bias:* How were factors like "customer retention," "brand image," and "investment attractiveness" defined and calculated? Was this identical for each respondent? Is the report measuring the same thing the same way in all cases?
- *Classification bias:* What made one respondent an ESG "adopter" and another a "laggard"? Where the line was drawn could make a huge difference in the performance measurement of the two groups.
- *Signal versus noise:* How were factors other than ESG controlled for? Many factors could have an impact on revenue growth, perhaps including some that explain the performance differential better than ESG.[4]

For Moore Global, a positive report like this could increase business for its ESG consulting services. "Moore Global can help your business meet its Sustainability goals through our unique Sustainability Framework," says its website. "Our framework is not only easy to implement and understand but can help you create fundamental change within your business."[5]

Publishing research that makes you look good is established market practice. In finance, we call tactics like this "selling your book" (as in a broker's "book" of shares). But even high-quality academic research has to be critically examined. The risk of spurious precision should never be assumed away.

That is why we now turn to a more promising source of truth for the link between ESG and shareholder value: a renowned publication called *From the Stockholder to the Stakeholder*, a "meta-analysis" that evaluates more than two hundred academic studies and sustainability sources.[6]

The report has a distinguished pedigree, as one of its sponsors is Oxford University. (The other is a sustainable investment asset manager, but the presence of Oxford is an assurance of the integrity of the research.) It made waves when it arrived in 2015. Endorsements rolled in from academics, corporate executives, and public policy leaders across the world. It still stands as a testament to ESG's power to boost shareholder value.

The report makes bold assertions: "We find a remarkable correlation between diligent sustainability business practices and economic performance. . . . 88% of reviewed sources find that companies with robust sustainability practices demonstrate better operational performance. . . . This report demonstrates that responsibility and profitability are not incompatible, but in fact wholly complementary."[7]

To find out whether the data lives up to the claims, I reviewed a number of the studies cited in the report for each of the three ESG "pillars"—environment, social, and governance—focusing on the ones that the text itself highlighted in making its point. I have picked one to represent each pillar, but keep in mind that others with similar flaws stand behind them. The reports cover a broad range of ESG practices, but almost all are alike in one important respect: They fail to prove the case.

Environment: Simplistic Scoring

The first paper that we will look at correlated a company's cost of borrowing to an environmental rating. In sum, it found that environmentally challenged firms pay more for their debt and are assigned lower credit ratings than firms with "proactive environmental engagement."[8]

Persuasive—until you look at how environmental performance is scored.

Imagine you took a course where your grade for the entire semester was determined by a single test, consisting of five true or false questions, equally weighted. Get them all right and you receive an A. Miss one, and you get a B, and so on. You might think that such an exam was too simplistic to judge your understanding of the subject. But this is how the rating agency cited in the study measured environmental performance.

A company received a score of zero or one on each of five environmental "strengths," such as "Pollution Prevention" or "Recycling." Each indicator was equally weighted, and no partial credit was given. The company also received an environmental "weakness" score, similarly structured, but with six indicators instead of five.

A scale this crude cannot possibly capture the complexity and breadth of environmental management. And even if the environmental performance of every company—from a steel mill to an online retailer to a hospital—could be precisely analyzed and cut into five distinct qualities, the relative importance of each would vary so much within each company, and from company to company, and from industry to industry, and from time to time, that scoring each zero or one, and then comparing those scores across all companies, would be a wholly arbitrary exercise.

Perhaps the most revealing part of the study was the subsection that looked only at highly polluting industries—paper, chemicals, oil refining, metal processing, and mining. The authors expected that lenders and raters would be most sensitive to environmental performance in the dirtiest industries, but their findings pointed in the opposite direction: "No incremental effect of environmental management performance on the credit standing of inherently [environmentally] risky firms." If environmental performance doesn't count financially in the industries where it matters most, it is hard to imagine it does in others.

Social: Reversed Causation

The study for the "S" pillar "analyzed the relationship between indicators of corporate social and financial performance within a comprehensive theoretical framework."[9] The result: "*No* significant negative social-financial performance relationships and strong positive correlations" (emphasis in original).

Again, a ringing endorsement of the social-financial link, but, again, with a twist in the tale. The study found that pairing social scores in one year with financial scores from the previous year produced the strongest link between social and financial performance. Switching it around, comparing financial scores one year *after* social ones, produced the *weakest* evidence of a relationship. Pairing social and financial scores during the same year had a correlation strength in the middle.

Rather than imply that social excellence leads to financial improvement, the data indicates the reverse: that companies with better financial results find they can afford to improve their social profiles. In accounting terms, social activity appears to be more a cost center than a profit center.

Governance: Where Are the Stakeholders?

The study for the "G" pillar looked at the correlation between corporations' governance scores and the coupons they paid on their bond issues.[10] It defined "governance" by grouping three hundred internationally accepted governance indicators into four categories.

- *Shareholder rights*, mainly "one share, one vote," that is, whether all shares have equal voting and economic rights
- *Disclosure*, whether the company publishes enough information for investors to make rational decisions to buy or sell shares
- *Board structure*, including the presence of independent directors—that is, without personal or business connections to the company
- *Takeover defenses*, whether the company could be purchased relatively freely or had implemented policies, such as "poison pills," that would impede its open-market acquisition

The study found that higher shareholder rights and disclosure are moderately correlated with lower cost of debt. It found no statistically significant correlation with board structure or takeover defenses.

But take another look at the "governance indicators." Is the study really dealing with corporate social responsibility at all? All the factors being studied are only relevant to shareholders. There are *no* items that reflect the concerns of other stakeholders, like employees or the environment.

This is not exceptional. Typically, research on "governance" analyzes relationships among shareholders, directors, and management—only. "Good governance" is usually equated with a balance of power leaning toward shareholders and away from managers and directors.

Logically, an activity with no direct effect on other stakeholders besides shareholders cannot be measuring overall corporate social value. "ESG" perhaps should be called simply "ES."

DEI: Ethical, Not Financial, Effects

DEI, standing for diversity, equity, and inclusion, was not treated as a distinct ESG factor in the meta-analysis because the term only grew popular after the study appeared, in the early 2020s, with the rise in social activism spurred by the death of George Floyd (see chapter 13).

As the term gained momentum, the SRI industry tried to make the case with empirical evidence that DEI, especially diversity, was a profit-driver. But these papers have largely been debunked. BlackRock, for example, published a blockbuster study in 2023 on gender diversity[11] claiming that financial outperformance could be correlated to four factors:

- firm-wide gender parity
- middle management diversity at the same level as firm-wide diversity
- women proportionately represented at higher ranks
- longer maternity leave

A noted researcher ripped apart the BlackRock study,[12] pointing out the following flaws, among others:

- Each of the four claims used a different financial measure, suggesting cherry-picking. A basket of financial indicators, consistent across all claims, would have been best practice.
- None of the claims had extensive controls (three had none at all) to account for factors other than the one being measured.
- The second claim was logically absurd—a company with zero firm-wide diversity and thus zero middle management diversity would be classed as among the best performers.
- Spotlighting maternity leave in isolation—why not paternity leave, for example, or other benefits?—arouses suspicion that this one indicator gave researchers the results they were looking for.

As for equity and inclusion, research on their effects on financial performance is scarce, because the words lack standard definition. One highly regarded study[13] found a positive correlation, but it did so by measuring E&I as a function of employees' subjective responses to statements like "This is a psychologically and emotionally healthy place to work," rather than objective data showing the presence or absence of distinct factors that could be precisely identified as "equity" or "inclusion." The study only proves that employees who feel good about their work environment are more productive. Transforming this commonsense observation into empirical evidence of equity and inclusion is a stretch.

DEI has real worth, but it falls outside the realm of finance. As the researcher who demolished the BlackRock study stated, "Even without a business case for diversity, there are strong moral and ethical cases. Some people argue that you should choose the best person for the job, regardless of characteristics. However, others believe that, due to systemic and chronic discrimination against minorities, companies have a role to play in levelling up by actively recruiting under-represented groups."[14]

In sum, ESG rests on the premise that certain types of socially positive behavior at a company heighten financial performance. But the empirical evidence, even in high quality studies, is shaky at best. Proving the thesis would require that these behaviors be chopped into specific actions, defined identically across all companies, measured precisely, and—most important—assigned a value. My practical experience as a socially responsible fund manager for many years reinforces my conclusion from reviewing the literature: In the final analysis, it is simply not realistic to say, "Here is a unit of ESG; it is worth this much."

9 ESG Funds Are Market Funds in Disguise

If ESG is real, then companies with more of it should have better financial performance, which typically gets reflected in better stock prices. Thus, funds that invest in companies with high ESG scores should deliver above-average financial returns. The financial term for returns that beat the market is "alpha."

There is a lively debate in the finance industry over whether ESG generates alpha. While much of the "research" on the topic is self-interested and promotional, we can also find valid, disinterested academic research.

One of the finest examples of the latter is "Have Investors Paid a Performance Price? Examining the Behavior of ESG Equity Funds."[1] This research paper appears in a respected publication, the *Journal of Portfolio Management*, and is extensive and rigorous. Best of all, is by two researchers who are not "selling their book" but rather arguing against it.

The two authors both work for Vanguard, the world's second largest asset manager with about $8 trillion under management. Vanguard manages many ESG funds, but despite their company's interest in encouraging ESG, the authors find that "the majority of environmental, social and governance (ESG) equity funds in any of the tested categories do not produce statistically significant positive or negative gross alpha." In other words, ESG funds deliver market-rate returns, neither significantly above or below.

Why are ESG funds consistently on par with the market? The reason is simple: Their portfolios are constructed mainly to mimic the market, not to maximize ESG ratings.

Let's do a case study to show how this works.[2] The subject is an archetypal ESG fund. It is one of the country's largest, $12.7 billion, and managed by the world's largest fund manager, and largest ESG fund manager, BlackRock. The fund is called iShares ESG Aware MSCI USA ETF and can be found under the ticker ESGU. The name is ponderous, but we can easily disassemble it.

However, the first thing to know about ESGU is that it is a passive fund, also called an index fund. All listed funds, whether they are based on the overall market or employ a distinctive strategy—like ESG, technology, or real estate, for example—can be categorized as either passive or active. Passive funds like ESGU eschew stock picking in favor of tracking a stock index, called the fund's "benchmark."

Some passive funds reflect their benchmark exactly, stock for stock, faithfully buying each share in the index in the same proportion that it appears in the index. This is known as "full replication." ESGU is a full replicator—the fund has 277 holdings and so does the index it tracks.

But full replication means relatively high transaction costs, since indexes typically rebalance quarterly to reflect the changing market capitalization of their components, and this triggers wholesale buying and selling by the fund to recapitulate the index. That is why some passive funds economize by creating computer models of selected stocks that perform in the aggregate in line with the benchmark despite having a relatively limited number of names.

The disadvantage of partial replication is that the models may not perform precisely like the underlying index. But even funds that fully replicate may deliver returns that diverge slightly from their benchmarks due to factors like the timing and costs of transactions.

The differential of a passive fund, whether fully or partially replicating, from its benchmark is known as "tracking error," and this is the primary basis on which passive fund performance is measured. Usually, tracking error is just a small fraction of a percent.

The counterpart to passive funds is active funds, in which managers employ proprietary methods to select the names and concentrations in the portfolio. Active funds also compare their performance to a benchmark index, but rather than track the index closely, they aim to outperform it, that is, create alpha. Since human fund managers cost more to employ than spreadsheets, the management fees for active funds are five times those of passive funds, averaging 0.59 percent annually versus 0.11 percent for passive funds.[3] And although passive funds tend to outperform active ones in the aggregate over long time periods, the best active funds can deliver superior returns, so investors who choose astutely (or luckily) are well rewarded.

With this background, we can interpret ESGU's name. At the back end, "ETF" stands for "exchange-traded fund." Like mutual funds, ETFs are collective investment vehicles, but are a bit simpler, as they can be traded like a stock whenever the exchange is open, incurring brokerage fees only, whereas mutual funds can only be cashed out once a day, at the close of trading, and may charge a redemption fee. ETFs are gaining in popularity versus mutual funds. In particular, passive funds are increasingly adopting the ETF form.

At the front end, "iShares" is simply a brand name for a family of four hundred ETFs managed by BlackRock, some sustainable and others not.

The middle of the name, "ESG Aware MSCI USA," is the important part, and it tells us two things: first, that ESGU is an ESG fund, and, second, that it tracks a benchmark index that belongs to MSCI, the world's leading provider of securities indexes. MSCI creates indexes and then leases them to fund managers and institutions to gauge their portfolios' performance relative to the index. Among MSCI's more than two hundred thousand indexes are many embodying themes such as ESG, geographic regions, or commodities.

(In addition to creating ESG indexes, MSCI is also a leading ESG rating agency, so it decides the ESG ratings of the companies in its ESG indexes. It maintains, of course, that these processes do not influence each other. As one of my former bosses in investment banking used to say, "No conflict, just interest.")

In the case of ESGU, it tracks an MSCI index called MSCI USA Extended ESG Focus Index (we'll call it MSCI ESG for short). MSCI ESG has two missions. One is to "maximize exposure to positive environmental, social and governance (ESG) factors." The other is to do so "while exhibiting risk and return characteristics similar to those of the MSCI USA Index." Like many ESG indexes, MSCI ESG also conducts a bit of negative screening, excluding tobacco, civilian firearms, "controversial weapons" like cluster bombs, thermal coal, and oil sands.

But what exactly is the MSCI USA index that MSCI ESG tracks? Here is the key: This index is a pure reflection of the overall stock market. It contains 601 stocks that constitute approximately 85 percent of the free-float-adjusted market capitalization in the United States. Its goal is to "measure the performance of the large and mid cap segments of the US market."

So let's recap. The fund, ESGU, tracks an index, MSCI ESG. This index tracks another, MSCI USA, which mirrors the overall market. Both ESGU and MSCI ESG do their tracking jobs well. The fund returned only 0.16

percent less than the ESG index over a five-year period, while the ESG index performance was only 0.13 percent less than the broad market index over a five-year period. Combining the two tracking errors, the overall divergence of the ESG fund from the broad market was just a few tenths of a percent.[4]

This double tracking ensures that the ESG fund produces financial returns very close to market rates. But ESGU is called an ESG fund, after all. Doesn't it deliver above-average ESG returns? Yes, but not by much. If we compare it to a non-ESG fund (Invesco MSCI USA ETF, ticker symbol PBUS) that directly tracks the *same* market index that the ESG fund tracks indirectly (MSCI USA), we find that the ESG score of the ESG fund is only 4 percent higher than the non-ESG fund. The funds also have substantially similar financial returns.

The reason that ESGU does not materially outperform PBUS in ESG terms is the same reason that its investment returns are close: The two funds' benchmarks contain most of the same stocks and in similar proportions.

Put the top ten holdings of MSCI ESG side by side with the top ten of MSCI USA. They are the same names, in almost the same order. The top three in both are Microsoft, Nvidia, and Apple. Overall, the holdings of the funds that track these indexes—ESGU tracking MSCI ESG and PBUS tracking MSCI USA—have a 98.5 percent overlap.

This is not by accident. MSCI ESG deliberately constrains its tracking error against MSCI USA to a maximum of 0.5 percent (and, as we have seen, in practice the tracking error actually achieved was materially less than that).

Half a percent of financial return does not provide a lot of freedom for the ESG index to vary stock selection in favor of high-ESG stocks.

The ESG index is not much more than a veil carrying the attractive name "ESG," draped over a straightforward market index. But for the honor of receiving slightly more ESG, investors in the ESG fund pay four times more in management fees—0.15 percent annually for ESGU versus 0.04 percent for PBUS.

The fee differential is not unusual. ESG fund management fees, including both higher-priced active funds and lower-priced passive funds, average 40 percent higher than non-ESG funds, 0.52 percent versus 0.36 percent.[5]

But is the fund in our case study, ESGU, exceptional in its paltry ESG outperformance relative to the comparable market fund? As a simple test, I took the six best ESG equity funds, according to *Forbes*,[6] paired them with non-ESG funds that tracked the same parent market index, and compared their ESG scores. The average ESG score uplift for the ESG fund in a pair was 6.5 percent, ranging from a high of 10.3 percent to a low of 0.1 percent.

All these funds are passive, but since ESG also features many actively managed funds, I looked at two large, well-established active funds, one ESG (Pioneer Fund, the same fund that invented negative screening in 1928 but has now adopted the ESG strategy) and the other non-ESG (Natixis US Equity Opportunities Fund). The result was virtually the same: a 6.8 percent higher score for the ESG fund.

Finally, since ESG asset management includes both bond funds and equity funds, I compared two major bond funds, one ESG (BlackRock Systematic ESG Bond Fund) and the other market-based (iShares Core US Aggregate Bond ETF). I found that the ESG delta in favor of the ESG fund was of similar size, 7.2 percent.[7]

While the dataset is small, the findings align with common sense. When you construct portfolios that are substantially similar to the market, you end up with not only market-level financial returns but also, necessarily, market-level ESG scores.

There is a good potential counterargument to all this. As we have seen, ESG funds ensure market-rate returns by tracking market indexes, to the point of deliberately constraining the ESG values of their components. But what if a fund cast aside the handcuffs of benchmarks and invested with the sole criterion of populating the portfolio with stocks having the highest ESG scores? A "pure play" ESG fund would constitute a litmus test of ESG's effect on stock price valuation.

A clever study did just that, assembling a virtual portfolio with long positions in each stock in the highest 30 percent of ESG rankings, combined with short positions—betting on price decline—in the lowest 30 percent. A "long-short" portfolio strategy is very common in fund management.

The study looked backward at the performance of the virtual portfolio over the previous thirteen years and found a significant improvement in raw returns over the market, 1.29 percent annualized. But the portfolio was heavily weighted in favor of tech stocks, since technology companies often score high ESG ratings, as they are "cleaner" than sectors like heavy industry or fossil fuels.

When the portfolio was rebalanced, keeping the same high ESG stocks but allocating to industry sectors in line with their size in the overall market, the alpha turned *negative*, minus 0.58 percent compared to market returns.[8]

In sum, listed ESG funds typically offer portfolios that substantially mimic non-ESG broad market funds. As a consequence, they generate financial returns, and ESG returns, at market levels. By failing to double down on ESG, they don't deliver the higher levels of corporate social responsibility that presumably would go with higher ESG ratings. Neither do they provide a test of whether ESG actually works to increase stock prices or not.

Research that does what the funds do not—measures the effect of ESG without the artificial limitation of index tracking—indicates that instead of boosting investment returns, ESG may actually *lower* valuation, after normalizing to give the appropriate weight to each industry sector.

This result should not be surprising. Finance has traditionally assumed that corporate social responsibility doesn't come free. Companies that maximize profits can't simultaneously maximize social returns, and vice versa. So while ESG tries to refute the old belief in a social-financial trade-off, its own performance tends to confirm it.

As the saying goes, *plus ça change, plus c'est la même chose*.

10 What Do ESG Ratings Rate?

ESG company ratings are the heart of ESG asset management, as they drive the selection of stocks in ESG funds and portfolios. ESG ratings have become a big business of their own, with global revenues estimated at $1.3 billion.[1]

Customers pay up for the products. Professional investors spend an average of $270,000 per year on ratings reports. Publicly listed companies spend even more, an average of $350,000 annually.[2]

But what do ESG rating agencies actually rate?

We know they attempt to rate a company's management of ESG risks. But not all of those risks—only those that affect the rated company's bottom line.

Take McDonald's Corp.,[3] which was responsible in 2019 for 54 million tons of CO_2 (or equivalent) emissions, more than the entire country of Portugal. This is largely because it is one of the world's largest buyers of beef, and cows release a lot of methane as they digest. The meat goes into Big Macs, and the methane goes into the atmosphere, where it plays a far more potent role in warming the climate, pound for pound, than CO_2.

The industry's leading ratings agency, MSCI, upgraded McDonald's ESG score in 2019, in large part due to a higher environmental score. Not because Mickey D's had decreased emissions. On the contrary, they had been on the rise for years. But this negative externality stays off the balance sheet, so MSCI ignored it.

Instead, MSCI credited the company with installing recycling bins in its outlets in France and the United Kingdom. This was a regulatory requirement to encourage customers to recycle. But in the eyes of MSCI, it constituted superior environmental management and should be rewarded with an ESG upgrade—ka-ching!

McDonalds is not alone in earning higher environmental scores while spewing ever-larger amounts of carbon into the air. Of the forty corporations whose ESG ratings were boosted largely on the back of better environmental performance, only one was credited with emissions reduction.

In fact, environmental concerns are so immaterial to most companies' profitability that "E" was the factor cited *least* often in a sample of 155 ESG upgrades, 26 percent. "S" had 32 percent, and "G" was the most prevalent, with 42 percent. (And, as we have seen, "G" isn't even a measure of corporate social responsibility.)

But the most powerful factor of all did not require companies to take *any* action, because about half the rating upgrades were the result of the rating agency itself becoming more generous in the way it assessed company performance.

ESG rating agencies diverge widely in their scores, especially compared with bond rating agencies. Bond raters use transparent analytical techniques like financial ratios and historical default rates to assess a company's credit risk. The result is that the bond rating agencies give bond buyers consistent advice: The correlation between the ratings from two leading agencies is 90 percent.[4]

By contrast, the correlation between two leading ESG rating agencies is only 40 percent. The lack of agreement is even more pronounced when breaking down their scores on each of the "E," "S," and "G" pillars—29 percent, 19 percent, and 16 percent, respectively.[5]

How is an investor to decide, for example, the true social value of Apple when one major ESG rating agency awards it an 85 (on a 0–100 scale), while another rater, equally major, punishes it with a 20? Similarly, scores for Meta range from 15 to 75, JPMorgan Chase from 30 to 90, and Berkshire Hathaway from 10 to 45.[6]

Part of the divergence comes from the inherent subjectivity of many of the factors evaluated by rating agencies. The agencies use quantitative analysis when they can, but factors like "community relations" and "controversial sourcing" cannot be expressed easily in formulas.

But more importantly, agencies come up with different ratings because they disagree on the very nature of the phenomenon they are trying to evaluate.

MSCI, for example, takes a bottom-up approach. A company rating is created by adding up a number of individual risk scores. MSCI selects risks that it thinks are relevant to the company and then grades the company's performance on each one, with higher grades given for better management. Each grade is then weighted, and the sum of all is the final rating, which is converted to a letter score, like a bond rating agency, from CCC to AAA. MSCI grades from two to seven risks from the "E" pillar, also two to seven from the "S" pillar, and six from "G."

Sustainalytics, by contrast, looks top-down. It starts by measuring the entire spectrum of risk that a company faces and then divides the whole into two parts, manageable risk and unmanageable risk. The manageable risk is then further divided into two pieces, managed and unmanaged risk. Finally, the rating agency adds the unmanaged (but manageable) risk to the inherently unmanageable risk to come up with a total risk quotient. For Sustainalytics, lower numbers are better, as they are measuring the residual after all managed risk is taken out of the equation.

Even though ESG rating agency scores look almost random on a scatter graph,[7] a clever study shows a mathematical basis for the discrepancy. The study—after analyzing more than seven hundred ESG indicators, distilled from more than twenty-five thousand rating reports—finds that the variations can be attributed to three methodological distinctions among the rating agencies.[8]

At the highest level, rating agencies choose *different factors* to include in their analysis. This accounts for 38 percent of the total divergence, according to the study.

At the next level down, even when ratings agencies measure the same factors, they *measure them in different ways*. This second-level variation is the most important, accounting for 56 percent of the total divergence.

Finally, agencies that measure the same factors in the same ways *assign different weights* to them. However, this only accounts for 6 percent of the total variation.

The crazy quilt of ESG ratings recalls the tale of the three blind wisemen who were sent off by the king to examine an elephant, the first ever to appear in the country. The first grabbed the trunk. "The elephant is like a giant snake," he announced. The second put his arms around the leg. "The elephant is like a tree," he asserted. The third rubbed his hand over the flank. "The elephant is like a wall," he declared.

Like the elephant, ESG ratings can appear very different depending on the approach. And like the blind men, the rating agencies are unclear on what it is they are actually describing. But if they don't know, who does?

11 Social Shareholders Are Unwelcome in the Boardroom

At first, it seemed like a twenty-first-century remake of the biblical tale of David and Goliath.

A tiny hedge fund bought $40 million of ExxonMobil stock, a mere 0.02 percent of the oil giant, and then boldly issued a challenge to the company's board of directors, proposing to unseat four of the twelve members with its own nominees.

The response was swift and unequivocal. The haughty Exxon board termed the four candidates "unqualified" and refused to meet with them. Battle lines were drawn. Both parties began campaigning for the votes of shareholders (called "proxies") in the annual general meeting (AGM) to be held several months later.

Exxon was mighty but not invulnerable. It had disappointed investors for years, underperforming other oil majors by a cumulative 57 percent in the previous decade. The upstart fund, named Engine No. 1, said Exxon's malaise was rooted in its failure to address climate change. It explained the following to fellow shareholders:

> ExxonMobil has no credible plan to protect value in an energy transition.
>
> - ExxonMobil is [the] world's 5th largest producer of greenhouse gas (GHG) emissions. . . .
> - This is an existential business risk given that ⅔ of emissions come from countries that have pledged to reach net zero emissions by 2050. . . .
> - A refusal to accept that fossil fuel demand may decline in decades to come has led to a failure to take even initial steps towards evolution. . . .
> - A lack of successful and transformative energy experience on the Board has left ExxonMobil unprepared and threatens continued long-term value destruction.[1]

Institutional investors, who held about 65 percent of Exxon's stock, took note. Typically, institutions support incumbent directors against outside challengers. But this was 2021, ESG was on the rise, the United States had just rejoined the Paris Agreement, and institutions were eager to show their sustainability credentials. This was their moment.

The attitude of California State Teachers' Retirement System (CalSTRS), the largest education retirement fund in the United States and the eleventh largest public pension fund globally, was typical. Said Aeisha Mastagni, a portfolio manager in the Sustainable Investment & Stewardship Strategies Unit, "At CalSTRS we are developing the idea of 'Activist Stewardship.' The idea is to combine our role as a constructive, engaged shareholder with deep financial analysis, while utilizing the full suite of activist tools available to address companies that are failing their shareholders and other stakeholders. ExxonMobil is our first example and it's hard to think of a better one."[2]

Both sides threw all they had into the fight for proxies. Exxon spent about $35 million to support the reelection of the incumbent board. Engine No. 1 spent almost as much to win over investors to their insurgent nominees.

During the shareholders' annual meeting, as Exxon felt its support eroding, it panicked and called a halt for one hour while it desperately phoned key investors for support. But the die had been cast. When the voting was over, the three largest fund managers in the country, BlackRock, Vanguard, and State Street, had joined forces, and others had followed their lead. Three of the current board had been ousted, replaced by nominees of Engine No. 1.

The social finance community hailed the victory. "Exxon's Board Defeat Signals the Rise of Social-Good Activists," announced the *New York Times*.[3] The world waited for the lumbering ship of Exxon to change course and start steaming toward a new destination in which fossil fuels would be history, replaced by renewables.

We're still waiting.

Engine No. 1 had warned ominously that global emissions reduction was an "existential business risk" for Exxon and promised that its board candidates would lead the company's transition. Yet its nominees seemed content a year later when board chair and CEO Darren Woods boasted, "ExxonMobil is investing more money to grow oil and gas production than any other US company."[4]

Exxon continued to double down. It bought oil producer Pioneer Natural Resources in 2023 for $60 billion, its largest acquisition since the merger with Mobil in 1999. With Pioneer in tow, Exxon's production from the massive Permian Basin in the Southwestern United States grew to 1.3 million barrels per day (bpd), twice what it had been.[5] In December 2024, the company vowed to continue increasing its oil and gas production over the following six years by a total of about 17 percent, from 4.6 million bpd equivalent[6] to 5.4.[7]

What happened? In a word, Brent. A world standard for oil prices, Brent crude, stood at $65.50 per barrel on May 26, 2021, the day of reckoning for Exxon's embattled board. A year later, Brent had climbed 57 percent to almost $103, reacting to the supply shock from Russia's invasion of Ukraine and increasing demand from economies recovering from the pandemic. Although oil prices moderated afterward, the average was still $86.36 from May of 2022 through the end of 2024, more than 30 percent higher than when Engine No. 1 joined the board.[8]

In addition, Exxon benefited from a loss of momentum in the global campaign for lower emissions. After a dip in 2020 related to Covid, CO_2 emissions from fossil fuels resumed their climb, reaching a historic high in 2024 of 37.4 billion metric tons.[9]

Exxon no longer imagines a world of scarce oil, if it ever did. The company projects[10] that global oil supply will remain at its current level, about 100 million bpd, at least through 2050. Critically, Exxon believes that new sources will have to be brought onstream for *more than half* of the forecast demand for oil, as existing oil fields are exhausted. And that is what Exxon does best.

If they come to pass, Exxon's projections point to a global catastrophe. To limit global warming to 1.5 degrees Celsius, the International Energy Agency estimates that by 2050, oil production will have to be slashed by about 75 percent from current levels, to about 25 million bpd.[11] A world in which oil continues to flow unabated at current levels indefinitely is a world that may be unlivable for many.

Exxon has not turned its back completely on emissions reductions as a new business opportunity, but its commitment to this, at about 17 percent of total capital expenditure, falls far short of transformative.[12]

Investors and analysts have cheered Exxon on as it rededicates itself to the oil patch. Wrote Morningstar equity analyst Alan Good in 2024,

> While many of its peers are diverting investment to renewables to achieve long-term carbon-intensity reduction targets, ExxonMobil remains committed to oil and gas. . . . It has responded to calls to bring in more outside voices to its board

> and announced emission-reduction targets. It's also investing in low-carbon technologies. . . . [However,] these efforts are measured and keep oil and gas production at the core. While this strategy is unlikely to win praise from environmentally oriented investors, we think it's more likely to be more successful and probably holds less risk.[13]

Institutional shareholders have also been quietly supportive as Exxon's stock price has surged on the back of oil price hikes, rising from $44.84 on January 1, 2021, when Engine No. 1 was preparing to breach the walls, to $110.15 four years later. For example, institutions have joined the board in opposing requests from social activist shareholders for the company to even plan for an energy transition, much less undertake one.

And the tiny courageous fund that saw no future in oil and gas? It has grown comfortable with the prospect that fossil fuels will be around for quite some time. After all, that is what made it rich.

> When we founded Engine No. 1, we set out to drive global change by running toward—not away from—the world's biggest problems. Sole reliance on fossil fuels is unsustainable both environmentally and geopolitically, and we need to continue to work to align energy development and use with the broader societal goal of decarbonization. [But] there are no simple or easy solutions, and *divestment from fossil fuels isn't the answer*. Decarbonizing the economy is a challenge but we welcome the challenge because we think within that challenge lies opportunity.[14]

In this version of the story, instead of conquering Goliath, David joins his side.

"Gadflies," Then and Now

The roots of shareholder activism go back to the aftermath of the 1929 stock market crash, when the newly founded Securities and Exchange Commission (SEC) imposed more transparency and accountability on markets and companies to restore the public's confidence in investing.

In those days, as now, publicly listed companies were required to hold AGMs and, in principle, open them to all shareholders to attend and cast their votes on key company matters. But in practice, many AGMs were conducted in a secretive and exclusive manner, and small shareholders were frequently ignored or dismissed. This rankled Lewis Gilbert, a proud man who lived off dividends from numerous minor holdings of stocks, wealthy but far from a tycoon.

Gilbert began to push his way into AGMs in the 1930s, despite being made to feel unwelcome, and agitated to increase "corporate democracy"—measures like dropping attendance barriers at AGMs and publishing their minutes, electing directors annually, and requiring shareholder approval for important decisions such as auditor selection and stock options for executives.[15] He was derided as a "gadfly" for his buzzing forays into boardrooms, but over time he managed to unite many minority shareholders behind his standard.

Over time, more gadflies joined the swarm, and their agendas broadened. In the 1940s, Wilma Soss, a public relations executive, fought for women to gain board seats and founded the Federation of Women Shareholders to organize the voices of women stockholders. Civil rights activist James Peck, who owned one share of Greyhound Bus Lines stock, struggled for years in the 1950s to end segregated seating on the buses and was beaten up with serious injuries in 1961 by a White mob when he sat in solidarity with Black people on a Greyhound bus.

As protest movements grew in the 1960s, activists occasionally targeted corporate AGMs to spotlight social causes. Busloads of protesters in 1967 descended on the AGM of Eastman Kodak Company, then a powerful camera and film manufacturer, to demand that the company train and recruit more Black workers. A year later, protests swirled outside the Dow Chemical AGM while inside shareholders debated the company's sale of napalm to the military.

Activist shareholders began nominating board candidates to challenge incumbents. In 1970 they mounted a drive to put three "public representatives" on the board of automotive giant General Motors (GM): an environmentalist, a consumer analyst, and a person of color. Although the effort failed, GM shortly afterward recruited Leon Sullivan, a Baptist minister and social organizer, to be its first Black board member.

Sullivan's influence extended far beyond his GM board service. His "Sullivan Principles," which became widely followed, called for multinational companies to end discrimination against their non-White employees in South Africa, even though this would bring them in conflict with the country's legal system enshrining White supremacy, known as apartheid.

In the 1980s, as social protest quieted, a new form of shareholder activism took hold, focusing exclusively on shareholder value. The vehicle for this was "hedge funds"—unregulated investment companies, open to wealthy investors only, that typically follow high-risk, high-return strategies. The rise of hedge funds was spurred by financial industry deregulation.

Under the leadership of "corporate raiders," activist hedge funds spearheaded hostile takeovers of listed companies perceived as undervalued. One classic example is the buyout of Trans World Airlines (TWA), one of the nation's largest at the time, led by financier Carl Icahn. Icahn was able to force the airline to borrow $540 million, in effect funding its own acquisition—a deal that led to Icahn pocketing $469 million. Three years later, in 1991, struggling with overleverage, TWA had to sell its prized assets, its London routes, to a competitor, and declared bankruptcy in 1992.[16]

Corporate raiding was a victim of its own success, and its glory days are past, as stock markets now typically accord fuller valuations, limiting the availability of raiding opportunities. But shareholder value activism is still vibrant, albeit on a smaller scale, seeking to find nuggets of unrealized value in target companies. The activist fund's usual tactic is to take a relatively small stake in a publicly listed target and then mobilize support among shareholders for seats on the board so it can implement measures like cost cutting, spinning off affiliates, selling assets, buying back shares, and increasing dividends.

Shareholder value activists are sometimes true gadflies, putting forth proposals that are patently unrealistic, not meant for implementation but rather to create an opening for a negotiation. While the talks may end in corporate policy changes that benefit all shareholders, they often conclude with only a deal for the hedge fund to sell its shares to the company at a hefty premium—in effect, a payoff to end a nuisance. This practice is known as "greenmail."

Only about 5 percent of all hedge fund assets under management are committed to shareholder value activism as a leading strategy, about $150 billion globally. But these activists punch above their weight in corporate governance terms. In 2023, activist hedge funds staged campaigns against 252 target companies, winning 122 board seats. As usual, they were particularly successful in the United States, where about half the contests were fought but two-thirds of the board victories won.[17]

Activist hedge funds succeed in creating value at target companies in the short term but destroy it over a longer time period, according to a study of more than one thousand activist campaigns in the United States.[18] The targeted firms' stock prices ticked up almost 8 percent in the first year after hedge fund intervention, compared to firms that were not targeted, but by year five, those same companies traded at levels 5 percent *below* their peers. The targets also lagged nontargeted firms in relative profitability and cash flow.

But shareholder value activists damage social performance even more than financial. Before they come into activists' sights, targeted firms have higher average corporate responsibility scores than their peers—categorized by community, diversity, employee relations, environment, and human rights. Two to five years later, however, their relative scores trail their counterparts by about 20 percent.[19]

Why Social Shareholders Don't Win

Social shareholder activists don't usually stage noisy protests at AGMs any more, but they are as active as ever in putting forward shareholder resolutions designed to improve corporate social responsibility. In 2024, social activists sponsored more than five hundred shareholder resolutions regarding E&S issues in the United States alone.[20] The leading social shareholder activists are social and environmental interest groups, religious organizations, socially responsible funds, individuals, and labor unions.

What do social activists ask for? A good guide is the annual report published by Interfaith Center on Corporate Responsibility (ICCR), a nonprofit alliance of socially responsible investors, most, but not all, faith based. ICCR does not file shareholder resolutions itself but coordinates its members' activity.

In 2024, ICCR members filed 344 resolutions, asking companies to consider actions across a broad range of issues.[21] The most important areas, ranked by proposal number, with examples of topics, were the following:

- *Human and worker rights:* Ensure living wages, paid sick leave, workers' rights to unionize, respect for human rights in supply chains, online child safety—75 proposals.
- *Climate change:* Accelerate emissions reductions; plan to transition to net-zero emissions—70 proposals.
- *Political contributions:* Disclose all spending on elections; assess political spending in light of corporate values; stop making political contributions—63 proposals.

- *Diversity and racial justice:* Close gender and racial pay gaps; disclose data on DEI—46 proposals.
- *Corporate governance:* Have asset managers assess how they vote at AGMs to ensure they are reflecting the views of their clients on issues like climate change—41 proposals.
- *Environmental health:* Reduce plastics use; assess the effect of operations on biodiversity; phase out excess antibiotics and pesticide use in agricultural supply chains—31 proposals.

If corporations had gone forward with even a small fraction of the actions these proposals contemplate, the corporate social responsibility landscape would look very different. But that is not how corporate governance works in practice.

Overall, shareholders of American-listed companies were presented with 525 E&S proposals: 170 (30 percent) environmental proposals and 365 (70 percent) social proposals. The result: Two environmental proposals passed—one asking the company to report on its GHG emissions and the other asking for GHG emission targets—as did only one social proposal, dealing with corporate political lobbying.[22]

The failure of E&S resolutions is even more stunning when you consider that shareholder resolutions—except for certain key matters like electing directors and approving dividends—are very seldom binding, in order not to infringe on the fiduciary responsibilities of directors to guide the company according to their reasonable judgments. The vast majority of shareholder proposals are "precatory," that is, a request, not an order. The resolutions ask companies to report, to assess, to evaluate, to plan—but cannot force companies to execute the plans.

Why don't more proposals pass? You need look no further than the fact that financial institutions own the large majority of shares in publicly listed companies, estimated at around 80 percent.[23]

Asset managers don't like to quarrel with the managements and boards of companies they invest in. Public disagreement could lead to a stock price downdraft, and recrimination might follow. Assets under management could flee. Reputations for calm, responsible stewardship could suffer. At the limit, the asset mangers' fiduciary standards could be questioned. It is much safer to sit on the sidelines and let managers and boards operate without impediment. Take the credit when things go well, and let management take the blame when they don't.

Institutions put up a show of active involvement with portfolio companies, what BlackRock calls "engagement." The world's largest fund manager reported that it held 4,000 engagements with more than 2,600 companies in 2023. BlackRock was pleased to find that "many of these companies demonstrat[e] agility in adapting their strategies and business models." To reward them for their agility, BlackRock cast its votes for company-supported directors in 89 percent of elections. It also joined with management in voting against 90 percent of shareholder proposals.[24]

Institutional investor passivity is not just a matter of convenience—it is a structural feature of the asset management industry. Take index funds. They are hamstrung because they have no choice but to buy shares in large companies in precise proportions corresponding to their capitalization in order to replicate their benchmarks. Otherwise, their holdings would be skewed in relation to the market, and their tracking error would rise. Any implicit threat by a passively managed fund to dump shares over policy disagreements completely lacks credibility.

Even actively managed funds, especially larger ones, typically hew closely to stock indexes rather than taking big bets in either a long or short direction. Smaller funds like hedge funds have much more freedom of maneuver, but the $150 billion that hedge funds manage overall only accounts for 6 percent of the $50 trillion US stock market.[25]

A few years ago, when sustainable investment was reaching a peak of popularity, institutions were more likely to support E&S proposals. But the bloom has gone off the rose, with increasing recognition that ESG does not produce above-market returns and growing opposition from right-wing politicians to "woke capitalism," as we will see in chapter 13.

BlackRock's support for E&S proposals fell from 40 percent in 2021 to 8 percent three years later. The number two fund manager, Vanguard, fell even further, all the way to 3 percent, but from a lower base, 25 percent. E&S support from the other two members of the "Big Four" asset managers, Fidelity and State Street, has also slid.[26]

Where the generals lead, the armies follow. Overall, asset managers' support for E&S was 15 percent in 2023, less than half of what it had been two years earlier.[27]

The complement to boardroom action is market action—persuading companies to be better social actors by divesting from companies that do not come up to the mark. But divestment is even more ineffective than social shareholder resolutions.

Divestment works in theory when a sufficiently large number of investors refuse to buy shares in target companies, lowering demand and reducing their market price. Currently, the most active and visible divestment campaign has fossil fuels as its target. According to the Global Fossil Fuel Divestment Commitments Database, which calls itself "the only comprehensive database of fossil fuel divestment commitments made by institutions worldwide," as of January 2025, 1,667 institutions had divested their fossil fuel exposures. These asset managers controlled about $40 trillion, or about one-third the global total.[28]

With such a large component of investors fleeing Big Oil, you would expect fossil fuel stock prices to swoon. But instead, they have been buoyant. For example, over the three-year period 2022–2024, an index fund tracking the S&P 500, one of the broadest measures of market performance (SPDR S&P 500 ETF Trust, ticker SPY), gained 28 percent. Another fund, managed by the same firm, that tracked only the energy sector of the S&P 500 (Energy Select Sector SPDR Fund, ticker XLE) had a performance over the period more than twice as good, returning 65 percent.

Another notable divestment failure is South Africa in the 1980s. Many institutional investors, including more than 150 universities in the United States and dozens of local governments and pension funds, sold their stakes in listed South African corporations, seeking a regime change away from apartheid. At the same time, many US and other international companies, including such giants as Exxon, IBM, and GM, ended their presence in the country and stopped trading with South African firms. (Terminating commercial relationships and exiting direct investments technically is known as "disinvestment," which is distinct from "divestment"—selling stock—but both actions are usually called for in activist campaigns, and called, generically, "divestment.")

Yet during this period, the Johannesburg Stock Exchange reached its highest levels ever.[29] Domestic investors had sufficient liquidity to absorb the shares divested by international players, and domestic capital markets were able to provide sufficient funding to replace capital assets lost through disinvestment. Ultimately, the strongest international push of apartheid down the slope to extinction came not from divestment but from the business decisions of international banks to withdraw credit lines, fearing political unrest.[30]

An Oxford University survey of many prominent divestment campaigns, including alcohol, tobacco, gambling, tobacco, and South Africa, concludes that *none* of them had a significant effect on the targeted companies.[31]

Deep, liquid capital markets are stunningly effective at gathering, distributing, and reallocating investments—an inestimable asset in generating value—but the flip side is that they are so robust and resilient that only an unprecedentedly large and coordinated effort by investors could translate social goals into stock price movements.

What is true for large, well-publicized divestment campaigns is just as true for the everyday management of socially responsible investments. Excluding a company from ESG indexes does not raise its capital cost, research shows. Neither does including the company improve its cost of capital. As large as SRI flows are, their effects are washed away in the public market's ocean of liquidity.[32]

12 Regulation: A Tale of Two Systems

"It was the best of times, it was the worst of times, it was the age of wisdom, it was the age of foolishness, it was the epoch of belief, it was the epoch of incredulity, it was the season of Light, it was the season of Darkness." So begins Charles Dickens's *A Tale of Two Cities*, a classic novel about London and Paris in the age of the French Revolution. The world of SRI regulation also evokes stark dichotomies, as the light touch of the United States contrasts vividly with the heavy hand of the European Union. Does one work better than the other?

The United States: Narrow Focus on Investors

Lax capital markets supervision in the United States contributed to the stock market bubble that popped disastrously in 1929. Regulation arose from the ashes of the stock market crash in a much stronger form, under the aegis of the newly created SEC. The SEC's mission is to build a robust framework of protection around investors by ensuring that companies provide complete and accurate information, that asset managers and advisors deal fairly and honestly with clients, and that markets function reliably and effectively.

In recent years, the rapid growth of SRI has raised concern about whether ESG funds are being marketed misleadingly and whether investors are being provided sufficient information about corporations' social and environmental risks to make informed decisions.

The SEC waded into the rising tide of ESG investment in March 2021, not by creating new rules at first but by setting up a Climate and ESG Task Force to better enforce regulations already on the books. The task force bagged some big names:

- Wall Street paragon Goldman Sachs Group, Inc. was charged with giving investors a false appearance of ESG propriety by ignoring its own policies in the ESG funds it managed. The SEC said, "The company failed to have any written policies and procedures for ESG research in one product, and once policies and procedures were established, it failed to follow them consistently."[1] Goldman paid a $4 million fine in November 2022.
- The US affiliate of Germany's largest asset manager, DWS Group, majority owned by German giant Deutsche Bank AG, was similarly accused of giving ESG only lip service. "As a firm, we have placed ESG at the heart of everything we do,"[2] the company said in its annual report. Yet internal documents from its Frankfurt home office obtained by prosecutors showed that it rarely screened investments for ESG. The head of the SEC task force, Sanjay Wadhwa, said, "DWS advertised that ESG was in its 'DNA,' but, as the SEC's order finds, its investment professionals failed to follow the ESG investment processes that it marketed."[3]
- In a heartbreaking case, the Brazilian mining company Vale SA was charged with falsifying environmental and social reporting with respect to the safety of its dams. One of the dams collapsed in 2019, killing 270 people. Vale fell under SEC supervision for having used US debt markets to raise $1 billion in debt. It paid a $55 million fine in April 2022 after the SEC took action.

In the Vale case, the SEC's head of enforcement, Gurbir Grewal, highlighted the link between investment decisions and social reporting: "Many investors rely on ESG disclosures like those contained in Vale's annual Sustainability Reports and other public filings to make informed investment decisions. By allegedly manipulating those disclosures, Vale compounded the social and environmental harm caused by the Brumadinho dam's tragic collapse and undermined investors' ability to evaluate the risks posed by Vale's securities."[4]

The SEC apparently learned from its experience with the task force that existing rules were not up to the task of protecting ESG investors adequately. It came out with a burst of proposals during a short period in 2022 to update and strengthen the regimen of sustainable disclosures.

- *Name rule:* Funds with characteristic terms in their names—like "growth" or "value"—have long been required to invest at least 80 percent of their capital in assets that correspond to those terms. As of September 2025,

ESG funds are subject to this rule. But the practical effect may be limited. ESG index methodologies already provide a clear description of what ESG does, and does not, include. However, investors tend not to give these documents a close reading, content with the "soft" meaning of ESG ("good for the world") that is prevalent in the public sphere.

- *Fund categorization rule:* Funds with social responsibility aims would be required to slot into one of three tiers.
    - "ESG-integrated funds": At the bottom level, if they used ESG as one factor among others to make investment decisions, they would disclose the ESG methodologies they used. They could then, in principle, be held accountable for implementing those methodologies in their ESG stock picks. However, as we saw in the chapter on ratings, a methodology is not a guarantee of accurately evaluating corporate social responsibility.
    - "ESG-focused funds": At the next higher level, funds would disclose greater detail on their methodologies. Importantly, they would be required to reveal how they voted on social issues at AGMs so that investors could determine if their actions in the boardroom conformed to their promises in marketing materials. If they considered companies' GHG emissions in their stock picks, they would have to calculate portfolio-wide emissions in a standard manner, known as weighted average carbon intensity, to make possible comparison among funds.
    - "ESG Impact funds": At the top level of social responsibility, funds would have the highest level of accountability and transparency, detailing the specific social or environmental outcomes they were targeting and measuring their progress against those targets, both qualitatively and quantitatively.
- *Climate disclosure rule:* Companies would have to disclose their level of emissions, and other climate-related risks, such as severe weather events, if they were "material," that is, likely to have a significant impact on operations, profitability, or business strategy. They would have to describe how their board and management were dealing with such risks, including the costs of mitigating them.

The proposed climate disclosure rule was intensely debated when it came out, garnering twenty-four thousand public comments from a wide array of companies and interest groups. While most commenters agreed that companies should reveal their roles in climate risk, fossil fuel companies and political conservatives mounted a fierce opposition.

When the SEC issued the final form of the rule, in March 2024, twenty-five states led by Republican governors and/or legislatures immediately filed suit to prevent its enactment, prompting the SEC to suspend the rule pending resolution of legal challenges. (The SEC has also suspended the fund categorization rule, as categorization is impractical without enhanced disclosure.)

Those who oppose climate disclosure have two main arguments, one technical and the other economic. First, they claim the new rules are unnecessary and outside the authority of the SEC. As SEC Commissioner Hester Peirce, a Republican, stated in denouncing the proposed rule, "We are not the Securities and Environment Commission—at least, not yet."[5]

The opponents point out that companies have long been required to report on material issues—and social and environmental risks are not excluded from this general requirement. In their view, the new rule needlessly and expensively expands the envelope of reporting to serve the interests of climate activists, not investors.

In response, supporters say the SEC is not enlarging the definition of materiality but simply refining disclosure requirements to reflect the growing importance of climate in the business environment.

The second argument goes deeper: It states that companies concerned about investor reaction to emission disclosures may prioritize climate-related issues over more important matters, putting shareholder value at risk. In effect, the dissidents argue that the more the market knows about a company's climate risk, the more it may force the company to do something about it—so the less it knows, the better.[6]

A stirring presentation of this view comes from the conservative think tank Competitive Enterprise Institute, acting as spokesperson for a dozen like-minded organizations, quoted in public comments on the climate disclosure rule:

> Politically, the function of climate risk disclosure is to extract confessions from fossil fuel companies that their business models are unsustainable in a carbon-constrained world. Such confessions could to some degree decapitalize and defund the companies, as investors and banks tend to shun businesses perceived to lack assets of durable value. The confessions could also invite litigation by

> shareholder groups claiming the companies committed fraud by overpricing asset values in the past. Such litigation could further spook investors and lenders, causing additional capital flight. As capital and credit ratings decline, so would the companies' ability to fend off legal and political predation. A death spiral is easily imagined.[7]

While overly dramatic, the warning points to a legitimate concern, for both fossil fuel companies and investors: In a world that bans carbon emissions, oil and gas companies have an obsolete business model. But if fossil fuel companies were sincerely worried about impending emissions constraints, instead of trying to hide the risks by killing disclosure rules, they would protect their interests better by starting down the path toward emissions neutrality, while keeping investors fully informed all along the way.

The reality is that such drastic warnings are "crying wolf," as carbon emissions are unlikely to be curbed significantly soon by legal measures—certainly not in the United States, where the second Trump administration, one of whose election slogans was "Drill, baby, drill," wasted no time in withdrawing the United States from the Paris Agreement on climate.

The European Union: Getting to Net Zero

In the European Union, SRI regulation is about more than investors and markets. A societal consensus reigns in Europe (although it has been fraying recently) that global warming is potentially catastrophic and adjustments are necessary throughout the economy, including the finance sector, to achieve net-zero emissions by 2050. To advance this objective, EU agencies have assembled a large package of reforms called the Green Deal, covering sectors like industry, buildings, transport, and agriculture, in addition to finance. The process is multilayered and due to be phased in over several years.

In the finance sector, the Green Deal mainly consists of two pillars, one setting high standards for corporate reporting—the Corporate Sustainability Reporting Directive (CSRD)—and the other imposing extensive rules on asset managers—the Sustainable Finance Disclosure Regulation (SFDR).

The CSRD originally aimed to pull in fifty thousand companies over time, including affiliates of non-EU companies operating in Europe. Importantly, these include privately held as well as public companies, in the belief that disclosures are as important for consumers and government agencies as they are for investors.

Under CSRD, companies would need to report on twelve "sustainability standards" composed of at least eighty-two separate items and 1,144 data points. They would disclose not just GHG emissions but *all* significant effects their operations have on the environment, as well as detailing transition plans laying out the path to net-zero emissions, complete with third-party verification of data and assumptions. They would also have to include their supply chain in the analysis.

Companies would also have to meet extensive social reporting requirements, covering topics like workplace health and safety, gender equality in the workforce, and even work-life balance. The disclosure topics also cover a company's impact on communities, from availability of housing to promoting civil rights and the cultural rights of Indigenous peoples.

The overriding theme of disclosure requirements is "double materiality," meaning both the effect on financial performance and social and environmental impact generally, even if unrelated to financial status. This sets the European vision far apart from the SEC perspective, which narrowly focuses on financial materiality and market efficiency.

Corporate executives have met CSRD with deep skepticism. A large survey revealed that very few think the reporting regime would improve financial performance directly. Only a minority of executives believed CSRD would lower cost of capital (32 percent support), grow revenues (29 percent), save costs (26 percent), or bolster competitive advantage (38 percent). Executives were more hopeful that CSRD reporting would boost factors tangentially related to profitability, like social performance, environmental performance, risk mitigation, and engagement with stakeholders, but most of these also garnered only minority support. Of all the factors surveyed, only one, environmental performance, won a bare majority of executive support, 51 percent.[8]

Stung by the critical response to CSRD, the EU began contemplating radical revision to the program in early 2025, such as substantially reducing the number of companies affected and the extent of the disclosures required, and providing much more time for companies to transition.[9]

Whereas the CSRD governs corporate reporting, its counterpart, the SFDR, applies to capital market participants. This rule, which has been substantially implemented, overlays a three-tier classification on all listed funds, whether ESG-oriented or not. This concept served as the inspiration for the SEC's fund categorization rule, but the European Union goes much farther than the SEC envisaged, especially at the top level of sustainability.

At the bottom level are funds without an explicit social or environmental mission, called Article 6 funds, often termed "gray." If the funds decide to adopt some measure of ESG in their stock picks, they must describe how they do so, but they are free to avoid ESG integration into their investment decision-making.

At the next higher tier are Article 8, or "light green," funds, which must state their intention to invest in some companies that promote social or environmental objectives. Although there is no requirement for a minimum percentage of socially responsible stocks in the portfolio, the required reporting on the fund's ESG profile is more extensive, related both to the fund's methodology and the assets they bring onto their books.

At the highest level are Article 9, or "dark green," funds, which are supposed to put *all* available capital into sustainable investments. To precisely understand what is meant by "sustainable investments," fund managers can resort to an official EU "taxonomy" that lays out in minute detail, both qualitatively and quantitatively, attributes that constitute sustainability.

The burden of proving an Article 9 investment "sustainable" is made heavier by the test of "Do no significant harm," which requires vetting against sixteen "principal adverse impacts"—fourteen mandatory, including GHG emissions, water pollution, hazardous waste, gender diversity, and pay equity, and two "wild cards" that can be chosen at fund manager discretion from a list of thirty-one options.

The SFDR, like its cousin CSRD, is not off to a good start. A survey of over three hundred organizations, conducted by the European Union itself, shows that a large majority (84 percent) of financial intermediaries do not think the SFDR disclosures help investors make decisions. In addition, a significant majority (62 percent) do not believe that the system strengthens investor protection. Slightly more than half (52 percent) believe it has no effect on increasing the flow of capital into sustainable investments.[10]

Most of the finance professionals (72 percent) concede that some system to categorize investments is needed. But they find the SFDR regime deeply flawed. The concept of "sustainable investments" is not clear (82 percent) despite the extensive and complex documentation around it. The data required to file SFDR reports is hard or impossible to obtain (88 percent).

These data gaps create legal uncertainty (79 percent) and pose reputational risks to asset managers and advisors (80 percent), while also increasing the risk of greenwashing and misselling to investors (81 percent). The European Union has taken the critique of SFDR to heart and planned to float proposals for revision in late 2025.[11]

The reality of the market bears out the harsh judgment of the survey respondents. Dark green funds made up only about 3 percent of the European-listed funds market and lost assets under management in 2024, while nonsustainable funds grew their capital.[12] One reason is that Article 9 funds underperformed materially with respect to their benchmarks. Light green funds fared better but still did relatively worse than nonsustainable funds—and also lost assets to the gray funds.[13]

ESG rating agencies, which follow their own methodologies, not the taxonomy of the European Union, are split on whether dark green funds have higher ESG quality than light green. Morningstar accords "above-average" and "high" ratings to a much greater proportion of Article 9 funds than Article 8 (combined score of 71 percent versus 54 percent), but another leading rater, Refinitiv, gives dark green funds only a slightly higher median score over light green ones (63 to 59).[14]

We can learn several lessons from the disparate experience of the United States and the European Union in regulating SRI.

First, about diminishing returns: Concepts like "sustainability," "socially responsible," and "green" are hard to define. Applying a complex, bureaucratic structure to the task may increase the workload without revealing much more usable information. Sustainability reporting is a classic example of a topic in which, beyond a certain point, the more effort you put in, the less progress you make.

Second, about the link overall between disclosure and financial performance: In the European Union, company executives don't appear to believe that required climate disclosures boost valuation or profitability. In the US case, the debate over climate disclosure is as much about principle as substance, since many companies voluntarily disclose carbon emissions and carbon tracking organizations make well-regarded estimates in the cases of those who don't. There is not much mystery about who is dumping CO_2 into the atmosphere and how much. Still, despite their culpability being widely known, fossil fuel companies have stock price track records, as we saw in chapter 11, ahead of the broad market.

If the battle in the United States is ever resolved in favor of more climate disclosure, both sides may end up puzzled about why they were fighting so hard.

Third, and most important, about investor priorities: Article 9 funds are, in effect, officially certified as socially responsible, yet they make up only 3 percent of the market. Their underperformance doubtless plays a role in this. By creating substantially equivalent packages—listed, liquid, diversified funds—that differ primarily in their contents—sustainable assets versus not—the SFDR has created a kind of "natural experiment" to test the extent to which investors are willing to substitute social returns for financial ones. The answer, so far, seems to be—not much.

13 "Woke Capitalism"

The rise of ESG, with its promise of greater corporate social responsibility, set off a spirited offensive from conservative politicians and commentators, who exaggerated its aims absurdly in order to score points against liberals. Here is a good example:

> The American free enterprise system is under attack from within. With the "Environmental, Social, and Governance" (ESG) movement, progressive politics has become a primary subject of corporate governance. . . . Some of the largest asset managers in the world have leveraged Americans' savings to coerce corporations to adopt critical race theory, boycott states with Republican governments, fund employees' abortions, and divest from investment in drilling for oil and natural gas, among a wide range of other left-wing causes.[1]

This fanciful depiction of ESG comes from *Consumers' Research*, a right-wing publication linked to the powerful conservative activist Leonard Leo. It is echoed by other prominent conservatives such as former Vice President Mike Pence: "The woke left is poised to conquer corporate America and has set in motion a strategy to enforce their radical environmental and social agenda on publicly traded corporations. . . . The shift is entirely manufactured by a handful of very large and powerful Wall Street financiers promoting left-wing environmental, social and governance goals (ESG), and ignoring the interests of businesses and their employees."[2]

Opposition to ESG—or at least the caricature of it drawn by some conservatives—has moved from rhetoric to action. Over the three-year period 2021–2024, 373 anti-ESG bills were proposed in state legislatures, 42 of which succeeded in passing, in nineteen states.[3] In addition, twenty-six Republican-controlled states sued the federal Department of Labor over its decision, during the Biden administration, to allow E&S factors as a tie-breaker in pension plan asset management.

The anti-ESG laws typically prohibit third-party managers of state pension funds, or other state assets, from taking into account any issues other than investment returns, both in picking stocks for portolios and casting votes at AGMs on behalf of state clients. Some laws preemptively ban investment managers that practice pro-ESG policies from contracting with the state. Many laws also include specific protections for the fossil fuel industry, barring investment managers from excluding oil and gas stocks in their portfolios. (Texas throws in the firearms industry for good measure.)

Firing back, five states, all controlled by Democratic legislatures, have explicitly given investment managers discretion to consider E&S factors in portfolio construction—but not at the cost of financial returns.

The debate is mostly political theater. As we have seen, ESG's core principle is that social behavior (at least some form of it) increases company earnings, not diminishes them. Even if they believed the opposite, no ESG asset manager would deliberately trade off investment returns for social ones. Right-wing activists either share the public misperception that ESG prioritizes social over financial concerns, or are deliberately misconstruing the effect of ESG for partisan purposes.

But playacting can have consequences. Anti-ESG bills put fund managers on notice that their choices will be scrutinized. They have a chilling effect on fund managers' promotion of social issues, curbing the willingness of investment managers to discuss the adverse effects of climate change in particular. They make it harder for fund managers to justify any relative de-emphasis of fossil fuels in their stock selection.

The success of anti-ESG bluster can be seen in the evolution in the thinking of Larry Fink, the founder, chair, and CEO of the world's largest asset manager, BlackRock, who writes an annual letter to clients with his perceptions of critical issues.

In 2020, Fink boldly stated that "climate risk is investment risk."[4] He added, "I believe we are on the edge of a fundamental reshaping of finance. . . . In the near future—and sooner than most anticipate—there will be a significant reallocation of capital."

In his 2021 letter, Fink doubled down. He pointed out that investment in sustainable assets was growing even faster than he had anticipated, spurting by 96 percent during the year. But he expected even more to come. "Net zero [emissions] demands a transformation of the entire economy," he said. And with change comes gain, for those who are astute enough to take advantage of it. "We also believe the climate transition presents an historic investment opportunity," he added.

Fink said the best way to realize that opportunity was to select high-ESG "purposeful" companies. "Acting with purpose enables a company to understand and respond to the changes happening in the world," he asserted. "Purposeful companies, with better environmental, social and governance (ESG) profiles, have outperformed their peers."

Fink's view of the future did not comfort friends of fossil fuels: "In the past year, people have seen the mounting physical toll of climate change in fires, droughts, flooding and hurricanes. They have begun to see the direct financial impact as energy companies take billions in climate-related write-downs on stranded assets and regulators focus on climate risk in the global financial system. They are also increasingly focused on the significant economic opportunity that the transition will create, as well as how to execute it in a just and fair manner."

But in 2022, apparently worrying that anti-ESG legislation might put investment mandates at risk, Fink moved onto the defensive. He wrote, "Stakeholder capitalism is not about politics. It is not a social or ideological agenda. It is not 'woke.' *It is capitalism*" (emphasis in original).

A year later, he continued to backpedal: "As minority shareholders, it's not our place to be telling companies what to do. . . . Oil and gas will play a vital role in meeting global energy demands. . . . We are working with energy companies globally that are essential in meeting societies' energy needs."

By 2024, the surrender was complete. Fink omitted the term "ESG" from his letter entirely and put oil and gas on the same level of importance as decarbonization, saying that "now the demand for clean energy is being amplified by something else: A focus on *energy security*" (emphasis in original).

The anti-ESG campaign fits into a larger movement by conservatives to suppress what they call "woke capitalism"—corporate social activity, either imposed from the outside by domineering financiers or arising internally. The term was coined in 2018 by conservative commentator Ross Douthat.[5] Douthat appropriated the word "woke"—which dates from the 1920s and had been used mainly to denote racial awareness—and joined it to "capitalism" to invent a label of ridicule for corporations that practiced meaningless virtue signaling, like refusing discounts to members of the National Rifle Association. Douthat's coinage was timely, reflecting the reality that pressure was building on corporations to take a stronger stance in favor of social and environmental goals, bringing to mind the social protests of the 1960s and 1970s.

The start of this cycle can be dated to the first election of Donald Trump as president, in 2016, which both reflected and exacerbated political polarization. A survey of consumers in 2017 found that two-thirds wanted corporations to speak up more on social and political issues.[6] But this sentiment was much stronger among liberals (78 percent); conservatives were almost evenly split (52 percent in favor).

Pressure on business to take a more progressive stand surged dramatically in the aftermath of the brutal murder of George Floyd, a Black man, by a White police officer in May 2020, which spurred a national wave of revulsion against racist policing and racism in general.

One month after Floyd's death, the board of the elite Business Roundtable, representing America's largest companies, formed a special committee to advance racial equity and justice. Many other corporations and nonprofit organizations joined Roundtable in the campaign. A total of 1,100 entities pledged about $200 billion in the year following Floyd's death to support Black communities, Black-owned businesses, anti-racism efforts generally, and criminal justice reforms.[7] "Black Lives Matter" became a nationwide rallying cry.

Another inflection point came in January 2021 when Trump supporters violently stormed the US Capitol in an effort to stop the certification of an election that Trump falsely claimed had been stolen from him. The influential pro-business organization US Chamber of Commerce homed in on lawmakers who voted against the pro forma ratification of Joe Biden as president, just a few hours after police and National Guard had cleared their offices of rioters. "There are some members [of Congress] who, by their actions, will have forfeited the support of the US Chamber of Commerce. Period. Full stop," said a senior Chamber executive.[8]

Two months later, many saw the threat to democracy continuing to rise in the form of a new law passed by Georgia's Republican-controlled legislature that tightened voter identification rules—with heightened impact on minority communities—and gave lawmakers more control over the conduct of elections.

Delta Airlines, headquartered in Atlanta and operator of the world's largest airline hub at Atlanta's Hartsfield-Jackson International Airport, was quick to respond. "[The] bill is unacceptable and does not match Delta's values," said CEO Ed Bastian.[9] At the same time, Coca-Cola, also headquartered in Atlanta, criticized the law, and Major League Baseball moved its All-Star Game from Atlanta to Colorado.

But the right-wing reaction was equally quick and unyielding. Mitch McConnell, the leader of Senate Republicans, retorted, "Republicans drink Coca-Cola too, and we fly and we like baseball. It's irritating one hell of a lot of Republican fans. . . . If I were running a major corporation, I'd stay out of politics."[10]

McConnell spoke for many conservative consumers. A backlash was rising against corporate social activism. About 40 percent of Republicans said in a survey that they would be less likely to buy from a company whose advertisements supported Black Lives Matter. Smaller, but still significant, portions of Republicans said they would spend less at companies whose ads promoted any of several other polarizing political issues: gun control, abortion rights, transgender rights, and gay rights.[11]

Wokeness Put to the Test

The contest between woke capitalism and its critics reached an apogee in early 2022, in a battle of giants pitting Florida governor Ron DeSantis against the Walt Disney Company, one of the state's largest employers and taxpayers—and also one its largest political contributors.

DeSantis championed a bill before the state legislature that would ban teaching about sexual orientation in public schools, nicknamed "Don't Say Gay" by its adversaries. Disney, a popular brand in the gay community, rated 100 percent on the Human Rights Campaign Equality Index, was appalled. Disney CEO Bob Chapek called it a "challenge to basic human rights."[12] Crucially, the company said it was stopping all political donations in the state.

DeSantis vowed revenge.

A month after the bill passed, DeSantis struck back, instigating the Republican-controlled legislature to strip Disney of special governance rights over a large district containing its theme parks and hotels—rights that Disney had held for more than fifty years, originally granted in exchange for its entry into Florida. As the company and the state lobbed lawsuits at each other, Disney seemed ready to wager its future in Florida. Many in the nation took sides.

But while Disney's defense of human rights appeared to show that corporate social activism rested on a solid base, in reality the foundations were made of sand.

Take Black Lives Matter, the largest show of corporate social commitment in decades. In the aftermath of the Floyd killing, America's largest fifty companies made a combined total of almost $50 billion of pledges to further racial equity and justice. But looking under the hood, less than 10 percent—$4.2 billion—was grant money, with the rest composed of revenue-generating loans and investments. The grants, mainly donations to nonprofit organizations in health, education, and community initiatives, represent only 0.2 percent of the combined net income of the donors, spread over five years. In a word, insignificant.[13]

In fairness, most of the 90 percent in revenue-generating activity appeared to be directed at mortgages for people of color or in low-income communities. Shrinking the homeownership gap between Black and White—which has expanded in recent years[14]—would undeniably be a social good. But the banks making these mortgages presumably intended to make money on them. And they did not pledge to return the profit to the communities where they were made. If the mortgage makers earned financial returns on this incremental activity, how did it differ from business as usual?

At least these fifty companies made a gesture. Of the largest three thousand companies in America, almost 80 percent of them did not even issue a statement about racial justice after Floyd's killing. But that is in keeping with their racial equity profile. In a racial justice assessment—covering both internal practices, like diversity and pay equity, and external actions, like community engagement—fully half of these large companies score below 20 on a scale of 0–100.[15]

Overall, instead of winning the confidence of people of color, corporations have gone *backward* since the dark days of 2020. The belief that "businesses serve the interests of my racial community well" has suffered double-digit declines among Black and Asian people, and only slightly less among Hispanic people.[16]

But companies are not listening to these communities. In the 2024 proxy season, one hundred shareholder resolutions were put forward at corporate AGMs on diversity and antidiscrimination topics, most asking for a racial equity audit to better understand the issues the companies faced and consider ways to improve them. Not one passed.[17]

Companies have abandoned the defense of democracy as readily as the fight for racial justice. Only two months after canceling lawmakers who had voted to overturn the 2020 presidential election results, the Chamber of Commerce was back in their corner. "We do not believe it is appropriate to judge members of Congress solely based on their votes on the electoral certification," wrote the group's senior political strategist.[18]

Following the Chamber's lead, the doors reopened for contributions to democracy-denying legislators. More than $18 million from more than seven hundred companies and industry groups flowed to members of this group in the year following the deadly riot at the Capitol.

Among the donors was a Ford Motor Company political action committee. A spokesperson for the company explained, "Our employee PAC makes bipartisan contributions based on a variety of considerations important to customers, our team and our company. They span things like manufacturing, mobility, innovation and trade."[19] Missing from the list of considerations: the Constitution.

In plain language, "Consumers have short memories, but lawmakers have long memories," said public relations consultant Gene Grabowski. "Doing business with the 'Sedition Caucus,' as distasteful as it might be, is a political reality for many companies."[20]

The cycle of corporate social activism continued to close after Trump won a decisive victory in his 2024 reelection bid. The war against woke capitalism, apparently won, was succeeded by an even more vitriolic campaign against DEI. Corporations were quick to salute the new flag. Even before Trump was inaugurated in 2017, nationally known brands like Amazon, Lowe's, McDonald's, Meta (which owns Facebook), and Walmart had ended, or cut back substantially, their support for DEI—a classic example of what students of authoritarian regimes call "anticipatory obedience."

And as for Walt Disney, the most steadfast of the woke corporate warriors? The valiant mouse has stilled his squeaks.

Disney decided in 2024, after two years of struggling with the dark forces of illiberalism, as the tide was turning, to settle its differences with the state. Both sides gained something. DeSantis did not give Disney back formal governance rights over its own territory, but he did agree to appoint a friendly face, a former lobbyist for Disney, as the head of the new government commission that inherited Disney's authority.[21] With her support, the panel granted the company relative autonomy for fifteen years, in exchange for a minimum of $8 billion in new investment.

For Disney, that is a low bar. Now that peace has been reestablished, the entertainment titan says that it plans to spend twice that much in the Sunshine State, adding a fifth theme park and fourteen thousand additional hotel rooms.[22]

The cause of the battle, "Don't Say Gay," remains on the books, though it has been softened slightly. While sexual orientation and gender identity are still banned from the formal curriculum, students and teachers in Florida may discuss these topics informally without facing prosecution.

Disney no longer protests against the anti-gay measure. More important, its wallet is now open for political donations. On the gift list are many legislators who strongly support the law that Disney once found intolerable.[23]

Other Approaches to Social Investing

14 Impact Investing: The Social-Financial Trade-Off in Action

Impact investing affirms what ESG denies: To be effective, socially responsible investing may require trading off financial returns for social ones.

ESG claims that corporate social performance boosts operational and market performance, although, as we have seen, this thesis cannot be sustained. Defining ESG quantitatively and measuring its effect on profitability precisely is a fantasy. In practice, ESG research and ratings don't deal with real financial factors, and ESG funds deliver market-rate returns mainly by doing nothing more than tracking market indexes.

By contrast, impact investing—a term that was popularized a few years after the origin of ESG to distinguish profit-first from social-first SRI—takes a more holistic view of corporate social responsibility, by investing in companies that prioritize specific social objectives over financial success. These enterprises must be financially self-supporting, at least—impact investing is not charity—but investors in impact companies should not be surprised if their investment returns are below market.

The expectation of subpar financial returns, coupled with the smaller size of impact companies relative to those in the ESG universe, are why the impact market is a minnow compared to the ESG whale. Impact assets are estimated at about $1.1 trillion, roughly equally split between developed and developing countries—about 3 percent the size of the $30 trillion ESG market.[1]

ESG funds and impact funds invest in very different kinds of assets. ESG invests predominantly in large, listed stocks. By contrast, impact funds mainly invest in small, privately held companies. Impact companies do things like distribute solar lanterns in areas where the power grid has yet to arrive, serve as crop merchants for small farms in underdeveloped rural areas, or lend small amounts of money to families to sell products from rudimentary stalls in open-air markets.

A company that puts social goals first does not maximize profits, by definition. And its customers often will be underserved communities that are hard to reach, require a high level of touch, and cannot afford high-margin goods. This puts major constraints on scale, making it unlikely that these companies can grow to a size that qualifies them for public markets.

Even if they could reach public market size, impact companies would find it difficult to reconcile their social missions with the exigencies of a listing. Unlisted companies have a great degree of flexibility, as they typically answer to only one or a few owners and are not required to publish their financial statements. Patagonia, a privately owned sports retailer, for example, "tithes" 1 percent of its gross revenues to environmental protection, was a pioneer in providing employee benefits like on-site day care, and helped found the Fair Labor Association, an independent organization that conducts surprise audits on suppliers to uncover worker abuse, including some of Patagonia's own suppliers. Patagonia even ran an ad in 2011 with a photo of one of its most popular products that read "Don't Buy This Jacket." The point was to invite consumers to reflect on the amount of natural resources that go into the making of every garment, and to buy wisely, and not too much.

But once a company has a public shareholder base, it is subject to relentless pressure to maximize financial performance and is forced to continuously hone its competitive advantage. The tyranny of quarterly earnings targets provides little room for gratuitous acts, unless the philanthropy is just a masquerade for marketing, like corporate sponsorship of high-profile artistic events. Capital markets don't applaud when companies give up even a small portion of cash flow or net income to advance social goals.

Patagonia again provides a relevant example. As a private company, its financials are closely held. But in 2013, a senior executive let slip in an interview that seventeen years earlier, the company had made an abortive effort to switch to 100 percent organic cotton, despite supply and quality concerns. "Our sales dropped 20 percent. It almost bankrupted [the company], especially the sportswear part of our business," said the executive.[2]

Patagonia fought back quietly and emerged stronger than ever from the crisis, but how would the markets have reacted had the shares been public and the financial reverses transparently reported? It is quite likely the stock would have plummeted, driving up funding costs, or drying up funding completely. Investors might have demanded a change in senior management and strategy. Competitors would have rushed in to take advantage of perceived weakness. Patagonia could have become a juicy acquisition target. The company might have morphed into something very different from the socially responsible and respected retailer that it is today, if it had even survived.

Another major difference between impact and ESG funds, besides the nature of the assets, is that impact funds typically provide fewer structural benefits to investors than ESG funds. Most ESG funds take the form of mutual funds and ETFs, which are large, listed, and offer daily liquidity. Their performance is transparently reported, their fees are low, and they regularly rebalance their portfolios to respond to changing markets. They are open to retail investors.

On the other hand, most impact funds are unlisted and closed-ended, meaning that investors are locked in for the fund's lifetime, typically eight to ten years. At the most, investors in impact debt funds—but not private equity ones—sometimes have opportunities to exit a portion of their capital at fixed intervals, called "gates," but there are no guarantees that the fund's liquidity will be sufficient at any interim point to meet the needs of all who seek an exit. The fund's assets are illiquid, after all. For the fund to retain a large cash position to accommodate potential investor exits would vitiate its investment effectiveness.

Impact funds are also typically much smaller than listed ESG funds, since the portfolio companies are relatively small, and so is their capacity to absorb incremental funding. Managers of impact funds often charge higher fees than nonimpact, for two reasons. First, the fixed costs of fund management are spread over a smaller base of managed capital. Second, impact investments—because they are bespoke and made in small, risky, unlisted, and illiquid companies—take far more time and effort to manage than a portfolio of securities in large, stable, listed, and liquid companies.

As they are typically unlisted, most impact funds are closed to retail investors by regulation. This cuts off a major source of potential market growth.[3]

To many investors, the most important distinction between ESG and impact is that ESG is designed to deliver market-rate returns, while impact investing is generally considered a below-market financial strategy. But is this perception correct? The answer is not obvious. Most impact funds are not required to publicly disclose their returns, unlike listed funds, as they are private, unregulated investment vehicles. But strong indications come from a comprehensive survey of emerging market impact funds, with detailed, anonymized data from eighty-three asset managers.[4] Its research shows clearly that, on average, impact funds in developing countries, whether debt or equity, underperform the market. There is no reason to believe that this is not the case in developed countries as well.

Let's look at the numbers for impact debt funds: The study finds that these funds deliver a financial return of about 2.55 percent annually in dollar terms. Since the risk-free rate, represented by ten-year US Treasuries, was 1.76 percent during the period under study, the funds generated a premium of 0.79 percent above that to compensate for the credit risk of the assets they held. But the median sovereign risk rating of the counties where the loans were made was Ba2/BB—a fairly low rating, below investment grade. Bonds with this rating were priced at an average credit spread of 3.37 percent during the same period.

This means that at market levels, the impact funds should have yielded at least 5.13 percent (1.76 percent + 3.37 percent)—and this assumes that the risk of the impact loans was as solid as the sovereign risk of the countries where they were issued. Instead, at 2.55 percent, the actual return was only half the theoretical risk-adjusted market rate.

On the private equity (PE) side as well, the impact fund yields were well below the risk-adjusted expectation. In practice, PE fund returns are highly variable, both in the developed and developing world. This is one reason why investors usually set a high return target for PE fund investments: around 20 percent annualized for a fund in a developed market, more for a fund in more risky emerging markets. However, the study found that actual returns for emerging market impact PE funds was well below that, at 5.92 percent.

Impact funds struggle to achieve market-rate financial returns because of a simple fact: It is hard to make a lot of money delivering goods and services to poor and vulnerable populations.

Here's a classic example, summarized from a case study.[5]

A debt impact fund lent $200,000 to a grain-processing company in East Africa to buy sorghum from several thousand small farmers in the neighboring area. The borrower processed the grain, resold it, and repaid the loan a year later, in full and on time.

The project was very positive socially. Not only did it link the farmers to an established source of income, it also solved an existential issue for them, enabling them to substitute sorghum, which is relatively drought-resistant, for their traditional cash crop of corn (maize), which declining rainfall had rendered no longer reliable. This was good news for everyone. Except for the lender, who lost 7 percent of the principal value, after netting out the cost of funds and operational expenses—on a deal that went exactly the way it was supposed to.

To help understand why good loans failed to pay for themselves, the consortium that the lender belonged to, the Council on Smallholder Agriculture Finance, performed an analysis of its members' lending overall. It showed an average loan size of $665,000—substantially higher than this example—and an average gross margin of 4 percent; that is, lenders borrowed funds at 2 percent, considerably below commercial rates, and re-lent them to borrowers at 6 percent. But all of this net interest income went to cover operational expenses—originating the loans, underwriting them, and servicing them. Factoring in credit losses of 3 percent—not very high in small-scale agriculture—meant the program was unprofitable.

Opportunities do arise to create material social value and full risk-adjusted returns at the same time—but not often. The CEO of a major foundation concluded, after twenty years of making for-profit impact-first investments (called "program-related investments" in the foundation world) that "while there is demand [from investors] for impact investments that create full market return and true social impact, these simply do not exist at scale."[6]

Despite the evidence, almost three-quarters (74 percent) of impact investors say they seek market-rate returns. The explanation, in most cases, is that they say what they must. About 70 percent of impact investors are fund managers, banks, pension funds, and insurance companies.[7] Many are fiduciaries, and all are commercial enterprises seeking capital to manage. They are bound legally, or at least commercially, to manage their clients' assets for the highest returns available within specified risk parameters. But for brand marketing reasons, they also want to appear compassionate and clued in to today's pressing social and environmental crises.

The result, borne out by my personal experience as a socially responsible fund manager, is that institutional investors tell impact fund managers, in grave tones, that they require market-level, risk-adjusted returns. And the managers nod, equally gravely, and promise to do their best to achieve this. But both parties know the odds.

To be clear, institutional investors do not squander their impact allocations. They examine fund managers' track records and skills seriously and go for best in class. But, in any case, impact allocations are usually an insignificant portion of total assets under management, so the relative underperformance of the impact segment is little more than a rounding error in total portfolio returns.

This constraint means that we cannot look to institutional investors to come up with the increased capital necessary for impact investing to realize its potential. Neither can we depend on the nonprofit or individual investor segment. Foundations, endowments, and family offices are a relatively small part of overall global assets under management and only account for about 3 percent of impact investment volumes.[8]

The most promising source of incremental impact capital is governments. Already, government agencies, called development finance institutions, provide almost one-third (29 percent) of impact assets under management.[9] Much of that takes the form of direct investment in portfolio companies, either in equity or senior debt.

Unfortunately, governments often compete with private sector impact investors in these deals. Alternatively, instead of displacing private investment, governments can achieve much more economic development bang for the buck by catalyzing it. They can do this by providing funding that takes on a disproportionate amount of risk, thereby lessening risk for investors higher up in the capital stack. This concept is called "blended finance." Studies show that for every $1.00 of such higher-risk finance in sustainable projects, an additional $2.50 flows in from private sector sources.[10] The multiple can be much higher in some blended finance structures.

Blended finance can take many forms. Here are three of the most common:

- *Loan guarantees:* By guaranteeing the loan, the government agency replaces the risk of the company taking out the loan with its own sovereign risk. Guarantees need not be for 100 percent of the loan's principal to have a "crowding-in" effect. Even partial guarantees may be rewarded by a multiple of funding from private lenders.
- *"First loss":* In a loan, or portfolio of loans, the government portion can be designated to absorb the first amount of any default. Like a partial

guarantee, even a small first-loss shield may have a leverage effect on private sector funding.

- *Subordinated debt:* As opposed to senior debt, which typically requires a pledge over company assets as security for repayment, subordinated debt is usually unsecured. This leaves more assets available to secure additional senior debt. In addition, the claims of subordinated creditors come after senior lenders in the event of default or liquidation, affording more downside protection to senior lenders.

The primary rationale for government support of impact investing is social value, not profits for taxpayers. Yet despite this, more than half of government development agencies say they are "market-rate investors."[11] Politically, this makes sense. It is hard for a government agency whose task is to make investments, not grants, to explain to lawmakers controlling their budgets why their return on capital is low, or even negative.

But financial return, of course, is the wrong metric to measure the impact investing success of development agencies. Impact investing, for governments as well as other impact investors, should be measured in social and environmental progress, not dollar returns. Unfortunately, however, as we see below, quantitative, comparable social value indicators are extremely difficult to put together.

Measuring the Unmeasurable

One of the biggest constraints to the growth of impact investing is the uncertainty of the size of the social-financial trade-off in each investment. How much financial subsidy—divergence from market-rate risk-adjusted return—does a specific impact investment deserve, in terms of the social benefits the company provides?

The sector could scale more easily, and impact fund managers could compete more openly for capital, if impact investors had a scorecard they could use to compare the "price" of each potential investment, in terms of financial subsidy, against its value, in terms of social accomplishment.

But measuring social value is like trying to grasp the breeze. A socially responsible fund manager describes the problem: "With climate, you can measure how much [carbon dioxide] is removed from the environment each year. Beyond climate, the units of measurement aren't as well accepted. How do you measure a unit of biodiversity? No one knows that. Something like education or poverty alleviation—there isn't an accepted measurement."[12]

The solution adopted by most impact funds is to relate their accomplishments to the Sustainable Development Goals (SDGs), a set of seventeen objectives for global betterment set by the UN. The SDG objectives are high level—the first two, for example, are "No Poverty" and "Zero Hunger"—but each goal is broken down into an average of ten targets, some quantitative and others qualitative. For example, in Goal 3, "Good Health and Well-Being," Target 3.1 is numerical: "Reduce the global maternal mortality ratio to less than 70 per 100,000 live births." Target 3.c is subjective: "Substantially increase health financing and the recruitment, development, training and retention of the health workforce."

The SDGs were adopted in 2015 with a fifteen-year time frame, but the deadline has proved too ambitious, and most goals have no realistic possibility of being met by 2030. The COVID-19 pandemic meant delay or even retrograde movement for several. Still, they remain official objectives for all UN members, and the UN regularly tracks their progress, forward or backward.

The advantage of SDGs for impact measurement is that they are universally acknowledged and comprehensive. The disadvantage is that they are meant for governments and cannot easily be adapted for business use. For example, simply operating a company and providing employment arguably works toward Goal 1: "No Poverty," Goal 2: "Zero Hunger," and Goal 8: "Decent Work" (assuming the company is not a sweatshop). Most companies would probably also claim credit for Goal 5: "Gender Equality" and Goal 10: "Reduced Inequality."

Some impact companies will get points for certain SDGs simply because of their sector. By definition, medical clinics address Goal 3: "Good Health"; schools promote Goal 4: "Quality Education"; renewable energy advances Goal 7: "Affordable and Clean Energy"; and affordable housing builds Goal 11: "Sustainable Cities and Communities."

The holy grail would be to standardize SDG measurement across all companies and industries—to create an "apples-to-apples" gradesheet so that the impact performance of a company or a fund could be assessed both on a standalone basis and in comparison to others in the impact space. With this in place, SDG alignment scores could be precise and reliable measurements of social value, as clear as financial indicators like profits and cash flow. But this dream is unrealizable in practice, as an attempt to do this in Europe reveals.

In the European Union, a subset of ESG funds has sprung up in recent years that attempt to quantify companies' contributions to achieving SDGs, and that use SDG alignment—rather than ESG scores—as a rating of corporate social value, and as the basis for investment decisions.

The European Union's financial regulator, the European Securities and Markets Authority, noticed the growing popularity of these funds and performed an analysis. Its principal finding was stark: "SDG funds do not significantly differ from their non-SDG counterparts . . . regarding their alignment with the United Nations SDGs."[13]

The regulator found that purportedly linking company actions to SDGs was so misleading that it could lead to "impact washing," that is, "funds making impact statements that are not backed by their investment strategy and holdings." It added, "This is mainly due to the SDG's broad scope, the absence of harmonised and standardised reporting requirements for private sector actors against the SDG targets and the inherent difficulty in assessing the extent to which a single firm can help contribute towards targets that were originally mainly intended for sovereigns."

The conclusion is that impact investing cannot be reduced to an off-the-shelf product whose price, financial subsidies, can be evaluated against its social value. There can be no substitute for examining each investment that aims for impact, understanding the mission of the investee (whether a company or a fund), assessing its unique performance, and arriving at a judgment that it stands or falls on its own merits.

PE Tries to Break the Mold

A number of mainstream PE fund managers are challenging the principle that impact-first investment is inconsistent with market-rate returns. They have entered the impact area with a splash, launching about a dozen mega-sized funds to invest in impact PE, with a promise that they will deliver the same full risk-adjusted financial returns as their other funds in their traditional developed country markets.

It is easy to understand why mainstream PE fund managers are charging into the impact space. With over $10 trillion of assets already under management in the developed world,[14] they are finding that competition for deals is intense, returns are eroding, and the environment for raising new capital is unpromising. Impact is a new land of opportunity.

Despite having little to no experience in impact, mainstream PE managers—names like TPG Inc., KKR & Co., Apollo Global Management, and Goldman Sachs Asset Management Private Equity—have amassed impact funds that are an order of magnitude larger than the sectoral norm. The median size of impact portfolios is $116 million,[15] but many of these new funds are $1 billion or more. The first of the new breed, TPG's Rise Fund, came in at $2.1 billion when it closed in 2017.

A typical PE fund has ten to twenty investments. If they follow this model, these billion-dollar-plus funds will have average investment sizes of $50–$100 million. Deals of this size are rare in the impact space as it has traditionally developed.

The new funds are booking deals, but unfortunately they disclose very little information publicly about their investments. However, some of the portfolio companies in the new funds appear to have questionable social credentials.

For example, the Rise Fund invested in C3.ai, an enterprise software company. The company's website says nothing about social impact but rather advertises that its artificial intelligence (AI) platform "supports the value chain in *any industry* with prebuilt, configurable, high-value AI applications for reliability, fraud detection, sensor network health, supply network optimization, energy management, anti-money laundering, and customer engagement" (emphasis added).

C3.ai is proud to list its customers and its products, including the US Air Force (predictive maintenance), the oil major Shell (industrial reliability), an unnamed "defense and aerospace conglomerate" (empowering supply chain teams), and a "global high-tech hardware leader" (accurate demand forecasting).[16] It is hard to imagine the East African sorghum processor we saw earlier in this group.

How does the Rise Fund justify an investment in C3.ai? By stating that its products "can reduce greenhouse gas emissions through AI machine-learning algorithms" and "can be applied to the healthcare sector to improve detections and interventions for diseases"[17]—though it provides no data on whether and to what extent this actually occurs. Still, this tenuous tie is sufficient for the Rise Fund to claim that the investment supports

SDGs 7: "Affordable and Clean Energy," 12: "Responsible Consumption and Production," and 13: "Climate Action."

The fund seems to be taking the view that any company generates "impact" if any of its products or services can be used, even incidentally, in a way that aligns with any SDG. Under this definition, it would be hard to find a company that did *not* meet the test. This is antithetical to the principle that impact companies should have explicit missions to further specific, named social and/or environmental objectives, especially on behalf of the poor and vulnerable.

On the plus side, mainstream PE managers are injecting billions of dollars into the impact sector and could bring billions more as they penetrate this market. On the minus side, PE has a shocking track record of destroying companies and livelihoods in an unprincipled quest for outsized financial returns. Mainstream PE corporate culture may taint rather than revitalize impact investment.

To understand this concern better, let's take a brief look at how mainstream PE works.

PE firms package capital commitments from investors into distinct funds with fixed terms. The funds buy majority stakes in companies and manage them for about five to seven years, and then sell them, return cash to investors, and dissolve themselves. Large PE firm have a number of funds in operation at the same time, each with $1 billion or more in assets and each owning and managing its own portfolio.

As they own a portfolio company for only a few years, fund managers have no incentive to show loyalty to the company's stakeholders—employees, customers, communities, suppliers, and the environment. The fund managers' exclusive focus on shareholder value is sharpened by self-interest: The fund manager typically receives 20 percent of all investment returns paid to investors above a minimum level (the "hurdle rate"). This compensation, called "carried interest," can be highly lucrative.

The gold ring of carried interest is a powerful incentive to discard any consideration but return on investment. The operating principle is to buy low, extract cash, sell high, and say goodbye.

In generating value for themselves, mainstream PE funds often do improve portfolio company financial performance. One study of over eight hundred PE-owned companies showed that their revenue growth was 12 percent faster and their operating income 18 percent higher than a control group of similar companies without PE backing.[18]

But PE funds sometimes squeeze their portfolio companies for cash too tightly, inflicting harm on employees and customers and even destroying the companies themselves. For a particularly ugly example, look at the US nursing home industry, where PE firms own about 10 percent of the market.

The mortality rate at nursing homes owned by PE firms is 11 percent higher than normal, according to an extensive analysis of more than twelve thousand nursing homes by the *Review of Financial Studies*.[19] This means that twenty-two thousand more people died at nursing homes owned by PE funds during the twelve years covered by the study, compared to industry norms. The study's clinical language understates the human tragedy of lives lost through poor care: "In the context of the health economics literature, this is a very large effect."[20]

The quality ratings of nursing homes bought by PE firms start deteriorating within the first year of PE ownership and continue to fall over at least four years. Deficiencies pile up, such as abusing patients and storing drugs improperly. Staff spend less time with patients. Patients are less active, develop more ulcers, and suffer more pain.

Despite crumbling standards of care, the PE-backed nursing homes bill 8 percent higher fees than average. But instead of going into operations, much of that flows straight to the PE funds in the form of "management fees." In addition, PE funds often force nursing homes to sell their facilities—presumably providing a nice dividend to fund investors—but then saddle the nursing homes with much higher costs to lease back those same facilities.

With fewer resources available to take care of patients, the PE-owned nursing homes are 50 percent more likely to diagnose incoming patients as mentally impaired and to place them on antipsychotic medication. Sedating patients is easier than caring for them.

The nursing home study shows, among other things, that PE firms have multiple ways of siphoning cash from their captive companies, including management fees and "asset stripping"—selling properties or other assets for dividends or fees. Often, the PE fund will have paid itself so handsomely during its ownership that it is indifferent to a portfolio company bankruptcy. Moreover, bankruptcy allows the PE owner to walk away from sizable current and future liabilities, such as employee severance and pension costs. This helps to explain why PE-backed companies are *ten times* as likely to go bankrupt as comparable firms without PE ownership,[21] including a number of nursing homes.[22]

It is sobering to think what this mindset could do to the impact sector. The only way mainstream PE fund managers could realize the social mandate of impact would be to thoroughly change the way they do business. But how likely is it that veteran PE fund managers, deeply skilled in cutthroat shareholder value maximization, regardless of social cost, will suddenly see the world differently after being put in charge of an impact fund?

The case of Bill McGlashan is instructive. He was a long-time senior executive at TPG in 2016 when he cofounded the Rise Fund, together with rock star Bono. He became known as an effective spokesperson for social capitalism, telling the audience at the elite Davos conference, for example, "Businesses go extinct if they don't get on the side of authentic good. We need to hold ourselves humbly accountable."[23]

But behind his supposed humility, McGlashan was a no-holds-barred operator. Shortly after he began directing the Rise Fund's social investment program, McGlashan paid a fraudster $50,000 to falsify his son's test scores to improve the boy's chances of gaining admission to the University of Southern California. He also was open to faking a photo of his son in football uniform to get him an athletic preference. "Pretty funny," an FBI wiretap caught him saying to his accomplice. "The way the world works these days is unbelievable."

A federal judge gave him three months behind bars and imposed a $250,000 fine. In sentencing him, the judge said, "Your enormous wealth, privilege and pride overwhelmed all of what you want to stand for, by your words and charity and philanthropy. . . . Here you are, convicted of a crime that displays an incredible lack of integrity, morality and common sense."[24]

But outside the courtroom, was PE listening?

15 Microfinance: Coping with Poverty, Not Curing It

Microfinance—small loans to low-income families in developing countries—is the poster child of impact investing. Who doesn't like the classic story of the poor woman who uses a microloan to buy a cow and then sells the milk, saves some money, buys a second cow, and then another, and ends up bootstrapping herself and her family into the middle class?

Microfinance is not only emotionally appealing; it is large—about 175 million borrowers globally and a total portfolio of about $340 billion[1]—and appears to deliver high social value to borrowers at the same time as market-rate financial returns to lenders.

As is so often the case in SRI, however, the reality is more nuanced. But to understand the inside story of microfinance, we need to know the basics. Start with this definitional feature: Microfinance is working capital. It is not consumer lending.

By "working capital," we mean money that goes into the short-term operation of a business: buying inventory, paying salaries, keeping the lights on. In principle, a microfinance loan is made to an individual, usually a woman, for revenue production: to buy fruits and vegetables for the market stall, to buy cloth for sewing saris, and, sometimes, yes, to buy a cow. (Although, strictly speaking, the cow would be a capital expenditure, not working capital, but the point is the same: business, not consumption.)

Microfinance is not meant to buy a television, repair the roof, send the children to school, or pay medical bills—as essential as these things are (except the first). These are examples of personal consumption, not direct revenue production.

In theory, the entire validity of the microfinance business model rests on the distinction between business use and personal use. Without a business to earn income, the underwriting rationale for the loan falls away. We will come back to this point later, but let's treat it as an axiom for now.

The microfinance borrower cannot get a loan from a bank. She has no significant assets to pledge as collateral, and her cash flow is small and uncertain. Besides, most microbusinesses are not legally established enterprises, with licenses, inspections, and tax certificates. They operate in the "informal" sector, tolerated but not approved by the state, and looked on with disfavor by banks.

Moreover, the borrower may be illiterate or at least unsophisticated. She would not feel comfortable at a bank, and the feeling would be mutual. The atmosphere at a microfinance lender—with its modest furnishings, friendly staff, and personalized service—is more congenial.

Globally, the largest portion of microfinance funding goes to retail trade—such as a simple market stall or a street food vendor. These are businesses with low capital costs and an inherently high level of robustness. The markup from wholesale to retail is hefty, and customer demand is constant—everyone has to eat. If flood or fire takes out the stall, the biggest loss is the day's inventory, and reconstruction is quick and inexpensive. The market woman can be back in business in a few days, if not overnight.

Ironically, even though agriculture in most developing countries remains the largest sector of the economy and the largest source of employment, microlenders—usually called microfinance institutions (MFIs)—typically don't make many loans to farmers themselves. The start of the food chain is the riskiest link—crops can fail in the field, be lost through disease or weather, or rot on the farm if timely transportation to market is unavailable. Crop prices are often volatile. At harvest, the increase in supply can drive down market prices. Small producers who cannot store their crops are vulnerable. Higher links in the chain—processors (like the sorghum company in the previous chapter), transporters, wholesalers, and so forth—are larger enterprises than individual farms and have more stable business models, and thus they are better candidates for microfinance loans.

The average size of a microfinance loan varies from country to country, roughly correlated to its level of economic development. In a poor country like India, where GDP per capita is about $2,100, the average loan size is $300 and the average microbusiness is very small, employing the borrower and perhaps a family member or two. In a middle-income country like Colombia, where income per person is three times higher ($6,200), the average microfinance loan amount is proportionately greater and so is the size of the business. Some borrowers may even have business licenses, pay taxes, and employ staff formally.

Lending methodology also varies with development level. In India, the largest microfinance market globally, with a total portfolio of about $40 billion, the standard protocol is the Grameen method (Bengali for "village"), initiated in Bangladesh in the 1970s by microfinance pioneer Mohammed Yunus, who won a Nobel Peace Prize in 2006 for standardizing and scaling microfinance (and was invited to become the interim leader of Bangladesh in 2024 after a popular uprising overthrew the authoritarian rule of long-term prime minister Sheikh Hasina).

The core of the Grameen method is forming a small "solidarity group" of women, typically numbering about five, in which each member agrees to take responsibility for the loans of the other members in case of default. The women undergo some education in financial literacy and the MFI's procedures before receiving their first loan.

The initial loans are quite small, have frequent repayments, often weekly, and mature in just a few months. Over several cycles of successful repayment, the credits grow in size and maturity, though the amounts remain modest and the maturities are typically under one year—reflecting their function as working capital. Microfinance is not designed for mortgages or financing expensive capital assets with long payback periods.

The solidarity requirement is more a moral than a legal guarantee and is rarely enforced strictly, but it is generally viewed as an effective motivational tool, especially in early cycle loans. Clients in later cycles with well-established businesses are often upgraded to single-borrower status, with no erosion of credit quality.

In higher-income countries, MFIs tend to operate single-borrower lending models, as the clients are more sophisticated, their businesses are larger, and their resources are more extensive. The moral suasion of a solidarity group has less salience. Additionally, the gender mix of clients tends to be more equal in more developed countries. Although globally about 80 percent of microfinance borrowers are women, this number is skewed by the large presence of India, where microfinance is almost exclusively for women. In many countries there is no gender distinction.

Some countries feature a mix of lending models. Mexico, for example, whose income per capita puts it in upper-middle status, has both single-borrower MFIs to deal with more well-resourced clients and solidarity group lenders to serve those deeper in poverty.

There is plenty of research, but no consensus, on whether women make better microfinance borrowers than men. A comprehensive study (1,200 MFIs, forty-two countries) presents good evidence that MFIs with more women borrowers have greater profitability and better portfolio quality.[2] But this study also reflects the outsized influence of India, a well-developed and reasonably well-regulated market composed almost exclusively of women. Similarly, there are multiple papers, but no empirical clarity, on whether being able to borrow increases a woman's status or power in society.

Many people outside the industry wonder why microfinance is barely present in developed countries. The reason is that microfinance fills a niche—individual entrepreneurs with minuscule amounts of capital engaged in unregulated commerce—that fades away as a country develops economically. The equivalent of a microbusiness in the United States is selling knickknacks from a blanket on a sidewalk. Fortunately, this sort of activity is quite marginal in our economy. Most people gain their living through formal employment.

By contrast, in most developing countries there is a huge imbalance between the working-age population and the availability of positions in the formal sector. There is no doubt that most micro-entrepreneurs would trade their tiny, risky enterprises for the security, reliability, and comfort of a paid job without a moment's hesitation. They are microfinance clients because they have no choice.

There is a joke in the microfinance industry that yes, we have microfinance in the developed world—it's called credit cards. True, a credit card balance, like a microloan, is a personal, unsecured, short-term loan with a relatively high interest rate. And some entrepreneurs in the developed world do run their small businesses on this basis—but move up to bank borrowing as soon as possible.

Well-run MFIs have loan loss ratios similar to commercial banks in the developed world, around 0.5–1.5 percent of their gross portfolios,[3] even though the apparent riskiness of their loans is much higher. There are four reasons for this.

First, microbusinesses are often robust and resilient. They operate at the lowest levels of the economy providing basic, everyday good and services with consistent demand. Their costs are low and their business models simple. In busy periods, or when cash is tight, family members can provide cheap or unremunerated labor.

Second, most borrowers don't depend solely on their principal business but rather have several sources of income, though these tend to be small and irregular. They can also depend on family members (or perhaps solidarity group members) to pitch in when loan payments are due. If the principal business fails to perform as normal for a period, there is usually some form of backup.

Third, defaulting on a microloan may cut off future borrowing. Although there is lively competition among MFIs in some markets, financial regulators are increasingly requiring the establishment of nationwide credit bureaus with comprehensive reporting down to micro levels, so that an MFI considering a loan can easily see whether a potential client has defaulted in the past.

Fourth, MFIs are often preferred over traditional funders like village moneylenders, whose terms are typically more stringent and whose collection practices are frequently harsh. A borrower will usually try to keep her standing intact with an MFI rather than resort to a less savory credit source.

Even though their portfolios perform well, commercial MFIs, which are the largest part of the market, almost always charge higher rates than banks. MFI lending rates vary widely, from near 90 percent per annum in Uzbekistan to just under 20 percent in Senegal, with a global average of about 35 percent.[4]

Microlenders demand higher rates for two reasons: First, microloans are expensive to service, relative to their size. Clients are often unsophisticated, live in remote areas, and need frequent interaction to maintain a productive relationship. Higher operating expenses for the MFI mean higher interest rates for clients.

Second, MFIs are not usually chartered as banks, and so they cannot attract deposits from the public or participate in the interbank market, both of which are relatively low-cost funding sources. Instead, MFIs typically have to depend on higher-cost alternatives like international impact investment funds.

Netting higher costs against higher revenues, MFIs are about as profitable as commercial banks, with an average 1.4 percent return on assets.[5] Their average loan portfolio is about $50 million,[6] though top-tier MFIs are much larger, some topping $1 billion. The international impact funds that lend to well-established MFIs earn an average credit spread of around 2 percent over U.S. Treasuries,[7] not far from a market rate, considering the relatively modest risk of lending to these organizations.

The Surprising Upside of Microfinance

Microfinance is a well-established, profitable, and growing asset class. But does it help borrowers?

The answer depends on the meaning of the question. If we want to know whether microfinance alleviates poverty, the answer seems to be no. For example, the US Government Accountability Office (GAO) analyzed nine microfinance projects by the US Agency for International Development and found that seven of them had no statistically significant results on the financial well-being of the borrowers. In addition, GAO did an extensive literature search and concluded, "Meta-analyses and systematic reviews that we examined generally pointed to small, if any, sustained effects of [microfinance] assistance to micro, small, and medium-sized enterprises."[8]

More specific evidence comes from randomized controlled trials (RCTs). The best way to study the effect of something, whether a drug or a microloan, is to conduct an RCT, in which a group of subjects receives the experimental treatment and a control group does not or receives less of it. In the microfinance world, these kinds of experiments are costly, difficult, and time-consuming, entailing years of observations in poor, often remote, communities. But about a dozen high-quality trials have taken place.

Most microfinance RCTs find little to no positive impact. For example, a meta-analysis of seven microfinance RCTs found that access to microcredit had a "moderate to high" probability of zero impact on households' income and spending.[9]

One of the earliest RCTs, still regarded as a landmark, provides a clear picture of the effect, or, rather, lack of effect, of introducing microloans into communities.[10] In 2005, an MFI, working with researchers, randomly chose fifty-two poor neighborhoods in the Indian city Hyderabad in which to establish branches. Researchers paired those neighborhoods with fifty-two similar ones where their partner MFI stayed away, though over time other MFIs entered both areas. The researchers conducted surveys, twice, of substantially all the households in all 104 neighborhoods. The first survey took place fifteen to eighteen months after their partner MFI had opened branches, and the second came two years after that.

Contrary to expectations, the study found that total borrowing did not increase despite the availability of microfinance. There was a transfer from informal credit sources (friends, family, individual moneylenders) to formal loans from MFIs but no net new credit.

In addition, the study found that longer experience with microfinance did not lead to higher standards of living. In those neighborhoods where microfinance came early:

- Residents were not more likely to start new businesses.
- The businesses already in place when microfinance entered the scene did not become more profitable, while those that started after the arrival of microfinance were *less* profitable.
- Families were not able to buy more consumer goods, like food, clothing, lodging, medical care, and transportation.
- Children did not attend school more or work fewer hours.
- Despite microloans being available exclusively to women, women did not appear to exercise any more influence over family spending decisions or priorities.

Taking out microloans did not appear to have a measurable positive effect on people's lives. But credit is not the only liquidity management tool that poor households need and often lack. Let's turn to another RCT for some surprising insights.

In a small rural town in Kenya in 2006, researchers approached women who owned and operated market stalls, offering to pay the opening cost of a savings account for them at the town's bank. The women would earn no interest on their deposits and would have to pay the bank's usual withdrawal fees. Nevertheless, 260 market women accepted the offer and opened personal savings accounts. After all, as about 90 percent of the women polled agreed, "it is hard to save money at home."[11]

Four to six months later, the results were impressive. The women with deposit accounts had been able to grow the amount of merchandise in their stalls by 38 percent. With the extra revenue, they bought 32 percent more food and 93 percent more personal items.

Simply being able to put money aside securely and access it when needed had given both their businesses and living standards a strong upward push.

But it is too simple to say that savings work and loans don't. In the Kenya RCT, men who operated bicycle taxis also were offered deposit accounts, but the outcomes were not positive.

Real life is complicated, especially at the bottom of the pyramid. But there is a clear underlying message: liquidity counts.

When bad things happen, poor people are less able to absorb the shock. Something as routine as a few days of illness can push a family into insolvency. A run of bad weather makes it impossible to work, a crash puts the bicycle taxi temporarily out of commission, a predator in the coop ravages the chickens—an interruption, even brief, in the daily process of getting by can lead to ruin. A small amount of cash when needed—be it credit or savings—could make the difference between coping with an emergency and being overcome by it.

But having recourse to modest amounts of cash on demand is not only about staving off disaster. It can also mean a material improvement in well-being. Buying screens for the windows leads not just to more comfort but more protection from disease. Replacing a frayed school uniform with a new one may give a child the self-confidence to persevere in a challenging classroom. A small dowry may give a young woman more discretion to choose the right marital partner.

This takes us back to the axiom that microfinance is working capital, not consumer lending. In reality, the liquidity needs of poor households do not divide neatly into two pieces. Understanding this, most MFIs do not strictly enforce the principle that loan proceeds must go exclusively for business use. The MFI in the India RCT put it well in their brochure: "Loans are used for cash flow smoothening [sic], predominantly for productive purposes."

Even though MFIs may not increase the total amount of credit in a community, they standardize it on transparent terms, and they provide it reliably and equitably. This makes microcredit a valuable tool to maintain household expenditures on an even keel in the face of volatile inflows and outflows, as well as dealing with stressful situations.

Microfinance succeeds as a business model because it inverts the hierarchy of credit risk traditionally taught to trainee lending officers in commercial banks. "The Three Cs of Credit" accords first priority to collateral—physical assets that can be seized and sold. Second comes the cash flow of the borrower, while character, in last place, is mainly a box to be ticked—you don't want to deal with someone disreputable.

But in microfinance, character is all, as poor people lack assets for collateral and their cash flows are insecure and unpredictable. In the final analysis, the basis of microfinance is mutual trust: The MFI trusts the client by making a loan, and the borrower honors that trust by doing all they can to repay.

Microfinance smooths cash flows for people in poverty, and in so doing it makes poverty easier to bear. But its value goes further. It shows that people who are materially poor can be rich in dignity and moral quality. And that is a lesson we can all benefit from learning.

16 Green Bonds and the Search for "Additionality"

Green bonds, so-called because their proceeds are designated for environmental projects, have become a large, global market, with about $3 trillion outstanding.[1] They are issued by a wide range of actors—governments, financial institutions, and operating companies—and are a standard feature in many portfolios. But although green bonds have funded many environmental activities, this achievement comes with an asterisk—because green bonds don't provide any financial incentives for green projects.

Unlike impact investing, green bonds don't ask investors for a subsidy. Green bonds are typically identical in their risk standing—senior and unsecured—to other bonds issued for general purposes by the same borrower. (The technical term for this risk equivalence is "pari passu.") The borrower's payment obligation is not tied to the specific risks or revenues of the green project financed by the green bond.[2]

Since green bonds are interchangeable from a risk perspective with the issuer's other general obligation bonds, they are quoted in the market at the same yield. Bond buyers have the best of both worlds—an instrument with the full faith and credit of the issuer, together with the public relations bonus of investing for environmental benefit.

Let's say a shipping company issues a green bond to replace its diesel trucks with electric ones. If the green bond is a senior, unsecured liability, as it normally is, the shipper will pay the same coupon on the bond as it would for any other general-purpose bond. But that means the return on the shipper's investment in the electric vehicles must be the same, at least, as any of its other capital projects. Otherwise, the shipper's return on equity, after repaying the bond, would fall and its creditors and shareholders would complain. In this case, the green bond provides no added financial benefit to either issuer or investor despite its designation for an environmental project. It is green in name only.

The same principle holds true in the case of a financial intermediary, like a commercial bank or state-owned development finance institution, that issues green bonds in order to onlend the proceeds for climate-positive projects. When it makes loans with the green bond funding, the bond issuer charges the end users interest rates that reflect their overall credit quality. If the issuer underprices risk in order to incentivize green projects—especially if it does so repeatedly—the quality of this portfolio will suffer, and it may have to pay more when it returns to the bond market, or be shut out entirely.

What green bonds lack is "additionality." This term refers to a quality that makes a beneficial activity more likely to happen. Additionality, in the form of an implicit or explicit financial subsidy, is what makes impact investing viable. Without it, green bonds cannot be considered impact investing.

Early in its development, the green bond market had an element of additionality. Investors were hungry for assets in their portfolio that they could point to as sustainable. The imbalance of demand over supply led to price premiums for green bonds, which lowered their yields. In theory, this market-driven benefit could have made room for green projects to be funded that did not have full commercial financial returns.

But green bonds have been the victims of their own success. As the supply of green bonds has risen to meet the demand, the price premium, called the "greenium," has slowly eroded. Currently, it is almost nonexistent.

In addition to additionality, green bonds lack accountability. In their prospectuses, green bonds describe the environmental purposes that their proceeds will be used for. But these clauses are not legally enforceable, according to a paper by several law school professors. The legal experts reviewed almost one thousand green bond prospectuses and concluded that "when the [green bond] issuer remains current on its payment obligations but fails to honor its commitment with regard to the use of proceeds . . . it would likely prove impossible to quantify the harm to an investor, leaving the investor without a damages remedy."[3]

But even though green bond issuers have legal uncertainty on their side, they are taking no chances. In 2014, all of the green bond prospectuses that the study reviewed made explicit, mandatory (in principle) commitments to undertake green projects. By 2022, only 30 percent of new prospectuses contained these commitments. The rest specifically *excluded* failure to use proceeds for green projects as an event of default.

Why are issuers so reluctant to promise that the money they raise with green bonds will be used to finance green projects? The law professors quoted a financial expert who worked with issuers on green bond deals:

> There is no issuer . . . not one . . . willing to bear the risk of legal liability [for failure to fulfill promises]. They would rather not issue than bear such risk. The premium the issuer would have to receive for issuing the bond would have to be much bigger . . . investors would have to take less in yield . . . right now, this is just feel good . . . PR stuff. I hate to sound so cynical. But this market exists because there are a bunch of funds who have to say they are investing in [green bonds]. . . . Analysts don't read this stuff. . . . No pressure to make credible promises.

Bonds with Additionality

Unlike green bonds, another category of SRI debt does connect the issuer's social targets to the bond's cost. Called "sustainability-linked bonds" (SLBs), these instruments commit the issuer to accomplish specified social targets within specified time frames, failing which the coupon steps up, usually about 0.25 percent per annum.

The option value of the potential to earn a higher interest rate typically gives the bond's price a slight boost. (The inverse is also possible, a coupon decrease in the event of social success, but rare—investors don't like falling yields, even for socially positive reasons.) SLBs are only about 10 percent of the market but still sizable in the absolute, at about $300 billion.[4]

Both governments and corporations issue SLBs. For example, Chile issued a sovereign SLB for $2 billion in 2022. The coupon will increase by 0.25 percent if the country's total GHG emissions don't fall by at least 10 percent, by 2030, and if electricity from renewable sources does not increase from 22 to 60 percent by 2032. Chile issued the bond at a yield discount of 0.1 percent compared to its customary cost of debt.[5]

In the private sector, an Italian utility company, Enel, issued the first SLB ever in 2019 and, encouraged by price premiums, went on to issue several more. However, in April 2024, the coupon step-up triggered on ten of its SLBs due to the company's failure to decrease its carbon emissions as stipulated. While the market responded positively, bidding up the price of the bonds to reflect the increased coupon, some observers were concerned that the incident may make future SLB issuers more conservative in their commitments.

The SLB market has been volatile, with charges that issuers have met the letter but not the spirit of the issuance. A 2024 survey of the market by the nonprofit research group Climate Bonds Initiative concluded that "the current SLB market contains a high share of low-quality deals that lack ambition, credibility, and adequate disclosure."[6]

Here's an example of the kind of deal that the survey likely had in mind.

Italian waste management company Itelyum issued a €450 million SLB in 2021. None of the bond's proceeds were invested in the company's core recycling operations. Instead, the money was raised to finance the buyout of the company from one PE fund to another.

However, the company did commit to two social performance targets in the bond prospectus. The first pertained to the company's main business of recycling machine oils and solvents. The goal was to increase the amount of emissions that the company would save from going into the atmosphere by recycling, compared to an equivalent amount of new products, by 25 percent over five years. The second was an increase over five years in the tonnage of total waste collected, again 25 percent.

Like most SLB issuers, the company hired a rating agency to provide an independent opinion that its environmental targets were "ambitious," a standard the market usually looks for. Typically, the second party opinions are clear and direct, but in this case the consultant was on the fence.

It said the targets *seemed* ambitious based on the company's historical performance, but it could not be completely sure because past performance data was not verified and could have been distorted by earlier acquisitions. As a backup, the agency sought to project the company's future financial performance based on comparable data from peers—but it could not locate any. The opinion was a masterwork of ambiguity.[7]

In any case, it was irrelevant whether the company met the targets or not. The coupon would not increase if the company fell short. The only consequence of missing the goals would be a slight increase, up to 0.6 percent, in the price the company would have to pay to redeem the bonds, *if* it chose to exercise its redemption rights. If it decided not to redeem, the bond would remain outstanding until maturity, *at the same coupon,* even if the company utterly failed to meet its environmental commitments.[8]

Despite its paltry level of additionality, the company's owners, PE manager Stirling Square, were very proud of the transaction. In announcing its closing, they said, "The bond received strong interest, with the book being oversubscribed multiple times, aided by its ESG features that attracted a number of socially responsible investors."[9]

The highest level of additionality in SRI debt can be found in a category, called "social impact bonds," that seeks to shift the burden of funding social programs from the public sector to private investors. The idea is ingenious. Bond buyers finance a state-sponsored social program, and they are repaid from the benefits these programs generate in the form of decreased government expenditure, or increased tax revenue, in the future. For example, a job training program that results in workers who resort less often to unemployment insurance and pay higher taxes, or a preventive healthcare program that that leads to lower medical costs later.

At scale, social impact bonds could reduce government budgets, leading to lower taxes, while maintaining, or even extending, the social safety net. But in practice, few social impact bonds have succeeded, and the market, estimated at about $400 million, has failed to take off.

Here are two notable examples.

Reducing recidivism: The City of New York wanted to lower the incidence of teenagers returning to jail after serving an initial sentence.[10] In 2013, the city's Department of Corrections entered into a contract with a nonprofit institute to offer a behavioral therapy course to about 1,500 young men, aged sixteen to eighteen, serving time at the Rikers Island prison, two-thirds of them on felony charges. The goal was to teach them life skills that would equip them to stay out of trouble with the law once they reentered society.

The course took participants through twelve steps, from "Honesty" at step one to "Choosing Moral Goals" at step 12, and included more than fifty sessions, though most of the inmates did not stay with the course to the end. The cost of the course, $9.6 million, was met by a loan to the city from Goldman Sachs.

The city calculated that if recidivism were reduced by only 10 percent from the average, the savings in detention costs would be enough to pay back the loan plus interest. However, the results went the wrong way. A control group—young men in prison who did not get the training—received new sentences averaging thirty-three days in the year following their initial release. But teens who went through training were imprisoned for four days *more* than the control group, an average of thirty-seven.

Since the city did not realize savings, it was not required to pay the expense of the course. But, fortunately for Goldman, Bloomberg Philanthropies covered most of the investment bank's losses with a grant, as this was a proof-of-concept project.

The evaluation report did not seek to explain why the training failed to reduce the teens' propensity to reoffend. But it noted that recidivism was highly correlated with the initial length of stay. Those who served more time in jail originally—presumably because they had committed more serious crimes—were more likely to spend more time in jail again. This was true even though they had been given the opportunity while behind bars to attend more therapy sessions.

Jobs for low-income youth: The government of Gauteng Province in South Africa awarded a contract in 2018 to a job training center to train two thousand young men and women and to place them in suitable jobs.[11]

The funding structure was complex. The $8 million cost of the training was met through social impact bonds issued by a special purpose legal vehicle. The bonds came in two classes. One, for commercial investors, paid an 11 percent coupon. The other, for nonprofit investors, paid rates that varied from 0 to 7.5 percent.

The reason for the two-tranche structure was to produce a blended cost of finance at around 7 percent, which was the normal rate that Gauteng Province paid in South Africa's capital markets.

In this case, unlike the New York City example, the training was successful. About 1,800 young people entered employment after completing the course. The government paid off the bonds, satisfied that it had received value for money.

But the third-party evaluation report was not so sure. It pointed out that the training institute had conducted similar programs for the government on other occasions, with similarly successful results. Were private investors really assuming much of a risk of failure? And if not, what was the benefit to the government of going through the exercise of funding the program by such complicated means, and without cost savings, instead of just taking it on directly as a government program?

In addition, the report noted that the training's economic value could not be ascertained in any case, as there was no control group. How many of the young job seekers might have landed suitable jobs on their own?

As these examples show, social impact bonds are complex. They depend on being able to analyze not only whether a social program is likely to succeed in making its beneficiaries more productive but also how much cash value that incremental productivity will generate for the government, either in foregone expenditure or increased tax revenue, or a combination of both.

Every case is a one-off, impossible to price reliably in the absence of any benchmark of comparable projects. Understanding, managing, pricing, and selling this risk is difficult, complicated, and costly, to the point that it can overwhelm the rationale.

These drawbacks mean that social impact bonds are unlikely to enter the mainstream of sustainable debt. They may have a role in attracting seed funding for novel programs where governments hesitate to fully commit. However, in such pioneering projects, it is probably more practical to seek funding through grants rather than elaborate, bespoke bond structures.

IV Climate: The Ultimate Social Investment

17 The Failure of Voluntarism

The facts are clear. Climate change is real and destructive. Its course will not change unless net carbon emissions fall to zero or close to zero. If this happens by 2050, climate scientists agree, there is a good chance that global warming can be limited to 1.5 degrees Celsius. The more this level is breached, they predict, the more catastrophic the effects, including droughts, floods, wildfires, sea level rise, more destructive hurricanes, debilitating heat, loss of arable land, and mass migration from areas rendered unlivable.

The stakes are existential, but business can reverse the momentum, as commercial operations are the source of most GHG emissions, from fossil fuels to agriculture to manufacturing. This makes climate finance the ultimate form of social investment. However, change is never easy. Transitioning to net-zero business models would force some corporations to undergo a radical transformation. Moreover, companies worry that extracting carbon completely from the economy could have uncertain and far-reaching effects. Some would win and others lose, but all would have to adapt.

Inertia is the preferred response of the corporate community, especially if your company or sector, like fossil fuels, has immense political influence and can stave off the threat of legal and regulatory mandates.

The result is that most corporations carry on with business as usual, even if pretending to show climate resolve. And SRI accommodates this, steadfastly supporting the status quo rather than using its capital to slow or stem climate change.

Many large companies, especially well-known brands, make grand statements about reducing emissions but typically do not follow through. A review of twenty-five of the world's biggest corporations—including household names like Apple, Nestlé, Volkswagen, and Walmart—found that *all* had made net-zero pledges, but *not one* had a highly credible plan to get there.[1]

The study gave twenty-one of the twenty-five companies scores of "very low" or "low" on the integrity of their net-zero programs. Only three were graded "moderate integrity," and only one, the shipping giant Maersk, got a "reasonable integrity" score, a notch below the top level of "high integrity."

To be fair, about half the carbon emissions charged to these companies came from relationships with suppliers or customers using their products. These up- and downstream emissions are called Scope 3. But the other half were under the direct control of the company: Scope 1 emissions, which come from company operations, and Scope 2, emissions from generating the electricity that the companies purchase. Yet the companies failed to present credible plans to curb most of these emissions as well. Overall, the study found that companies had convincing programs to reduce only 20 percent of their total emissions.

These companies, large as they are, only accounted for about 5 percent of total global GHG emissions (Scopes 1, 2, and 3 combined). By contrast, the most prolific emitters do not even pretend to aim for net zero, according to a study by the World Bank of 157 multinational companies, collectively responsible for 60 percent of global industrial emissions.[2]

The World Bank study said that only one-fourth of the mega-emitters had a net-zero target, and for them the main motivation for setting the target was pressure from government, not concern for a livable world. Even among those pledging allegiance to net zero by 2050, *not one* had a plan to allocate sufficient capital to achieve it.

The case of Big Oil is unique, as fossil fuels are responsible for over 90 percent of CO_2 emissions. But only 11 percent of this comes from their own operations—drilling, refining, transporting, and so on—and from the power they purchase from the grid. Most of the rest results when the fuels they produce and sell are burned.[3]

That is why many pledges from fossil fuel companies to reduce or eliminate emissions are misleading. For example, "ExxonMobil announces ambition for net zero greenhouse gas emissions by 2050,"[4] the oil giant proclaimed in January 2022. But a closer reading revealed that Exxon was referring to "operated assets" only, that is, Scope 1 and Scope 2, not the massively greater amount of CO_2 that comes from using its products. Rather than phasing out oil and gas production, as one might think from the headline, Exxon plans to *increase* it.

In Exxon's bizarre worldview, "net zero" would be when its refineries continue to pump out fossil fuels, more than ever, but get their own power from wind and solar.

For a while, banks seemed ready to force corporations into a climate transition. In 2021, the Net-Zero Banking Alliance was formed, whose members committed to "align lending and investment portfolios with net-zero emissions by 2050." At its peak, the alliance counted 138 banks controlling over 40 percent of global banking assets.

Yet, as in the case of the Business Roundtable's adoption of stakeholder value (see chapter 5), the promises were empty. Research shows that banks belonging to the alliance, relative to nonmember banks, do not reduce lending to carbon-emitting sectors. Neither do they increase financing for renewable power projects. As they don't enforce their pledges, their borrowers are not more likely to reduce emissions or set climate targets.[5] Moreover, banks collectively have *increased* their funding to the fossil fuel sector since the alliance was founded.[6]

The banking climate alliance has been decimated in the anti-woke backlash discussed in chapter 13. Six major banks from the United States alone resigned in the month preceding the second inauguration of Donald Trump. Similarly, other net-zero alliances of institutional investors have become obsolete. The Net Zero Asset Managers Initiative suspended its activities in early 2025, stung by the exit of BlackRock and other leading asset managers. The Net-Zero Insurance Alliance has been discontinued.

The departure of investor alliances should not be mourned, as their impact has been negligible.

Offsets That Don't Offset

Instead of reducing carbon emissions, companies are increasingly turning to a form of mitigation called carbon offsets, or carbon credits.

The principle is sound: If a company emits a ton of CO_2 but also builds a solar farm that produces enough electricity from the sun to replace a ton of carbon from coal or gas power generation, it is not making the world better, but at least it is not making it worse.

Carbon offset projects come in many forms and sizes. Although the most prevalent type is renewable energy production, offset projects also preserve forests, capture methane from landfills, restore marshes, pull CO_2

directly out of the air, and enhance soil's ability to absorb carbon, among other things.

Many carbon offset projects are genuine, especially those associated with government-sponsored "cap-and-trade" systems, as we discuss in the next chapter. But outside of mandatory systems, there is an unregulated Wild West of *voluntary* carbon credits, often marked by fraud and scandal.

While still in a formative stage, estimated at about $7 billion per year, the voluntary carbon offset market is projected to grow dramatically, to $60 billion per year.[7] The largest buyers of voluntary carbon credits, unsurprisingly, are fossil fuel companies, hoping to relieve public pressure on them to reduce their own emissions.[8]

The pitfalls of the voluntary carbon offset market are shown best in its fastest growing segment, which is also its most discredited: cookstoves. The need for clean cooking is imperative. Globally, more than three billion people cook with dirty fuels like coal, kerosene, dung, and charcoal over open fires or with primitive stoves. In sub-Saharan Africa alone, almost a billion people depend on firewood and charcoal for cooking.[9] Cooking with clean fuel would cut about 1.5 billion tons of GHG emissions annually.[10] It would also eliminate almost four million premature deaths annually from the carcinogens and other pollutants in the smoke that dirty fuels belch out.[11]

More efficient stoves can making cooking safer, easier, and more cost-effective, with less fuel, less smoke, less risk of fire, less harm to health—and less CO_2 emissions. The reduction in carbon emissions from lower fuel consumption and more complete combustion in efficient cookstoves can be calculated, packaged in carbon offset certificates, each good for one ton of precluded CO_2, and sold on a private, voluntary carbon markets exchange.

Cookstove replacement already accounts for offset certificates worth about 80 million tons per year of displaced CO_2.[12] But many projects are sheer illusion.

For example, in a survey of fifty-one projects, covering twenty-five countries, researchers found that the amount of carbon reduction attributable to more efficient cookstoves had been massively overestimated—by almost ten times.[13] The number and usage of stoves, the quantity of wood they conserved, and the amount of CO_2 emissions they precluded were all grossly exaggerated.

A case study from the *Washington Post* illustrates the lack of safeguards in the market. Reporters tramped through miles of Mozambican countryside looking in vain for households that used stoves they had received without cost from a manufacturer in the United States.[14] The US company had implemented a foolproof business model: Give away cheaply made stoves and monetize the carbon reduction ascribed to their use by selling carbon credits. The more stoves they unloaded for free, the more money they made from the stoves' supposed benefits.

But although the reporters visited hundreds of homes that had been given stoves, they found very few in use. The recipients said the stoves were not durable. Their clay brick footings crumbled in the rain, but using them inside (which was not recommended) produced thick smoke. Of the fifty-two households interviewed, only thirteen said they still had working stoves, and only three used them regularly.

Overstatement is the rule in the forestry segment as well, which is the second largest category of offset credits, after renewable energy. One study found that 90 percent of forestry conservation offsets were "phantom credits" and did not represent true reductions despite being certified by a leading private agency.[15]

Most of the phony credits came from counting emissions savings from forests that faced little threat of destruction, the researchers found. In some cases, residents who had lived for years within forests sustainably were forcibly evicted and their homes destroyed so that the forest could be deemed eligible for offset credits.[16]

Even long-established, respected nonprofit organizations can succumb to the temptation to make easy money by claiming that the properties they hold as permanent assets face imminent existential risk. The National Audubon Society, for example, collected $3 million in credit sales by promising not to cut down a cypress forest in South Carolina, thereby allegedly preserving 900,0000 tons of CO_2 sequestration anually—the equivalent of tailpipe emissions from almost two hundred thousand cars.

But the organization had proudly held the forest intact for more than forty years and lauded it on their website as "a pristine ecosystem untouched for millenia." The man who had managed the sanctuary for Audubon for decades confirmed the obvious. "We never intended to cut that forest," he said.[17]

What should be the easiest case for offsets, renewable energy, is actually the hardest, though not in a technical sense. Solar and wind projects have been standardized to a large degree. Calculating their output and converting it into tons of carbon saved from not burning fossil fuels is straightforward—much less complex than estimating carbon uptake by a forest, for example, which will vary significantly depending on factors such as weather, plant disease, and tree growth rates.

The problem with many renewable power projects that issue carbon credits is that they are *too* good; that is, commercially viable. A commercially sustainable project can finance itself with capital from the market. It does not need to issue offset carbon credits to operate. An investor buying credits in a self-supporting renewable energy project is not displacing carbon; they are simply displacing other investors.

Here, as in the case of green bonds (chapter 16), the issue is lack of additionality.

An analysis that scored over four thousand renewable energy projects in developing countries that sold carbon credits gave the worst grade—"low" likelihood of generating additionality—to *every one*.[18]

Even with good intentions, structuring and maintaining an offset project in accordance with best practice is complex and costly:

- The project must be additional—that is, require a financial subsidy to be viable. Otherwise, the carbon credit proceeds are futile as the project would happen in any case.
- The project must generate substantial amounts of real and measurable carbon reduction. That may be easy to demonstrate in solar or wind but harder in more exotic projects like wetlands restoration or livestock methane capture.
- The project must avoid "leakage," meaning displacing carbon-emitting activity rather than eliminating it. The classic example is when protecting a tract of forest simply pushes logging into an adjoining one.
- External verification and regular monitoring are critical to assure that projects meet requirements and are well maintained.
- The project should be permanent. This is perhaps the hardest condition to fulfill. Plant disease, machinery breakdown, severe weather, changing cost structures, personnel turnover, and other roadblocks to business continuity are a fact of life. The project needs enough layers of support to assure durability, adding to its cost and complexity.

Voluntary credits are traded on privately owned, unregulated markets. This creates a "race to the bottom" in which unscrupulous arrangers and issuers feed the demand of buyers who want credits, preferably cheap ones, to give them cover to maintain, or even increase, their own emissions. Private verification agencies face the temptation to ease rigor in order to attract clients.

The only way to bring order and stability to the market would be through regulation. But standardizing and overseeing such a complex and varied set of activities would be daunting and expensive. Nevertheless, governments are starting to circle around the issue. In the United States, for example, although the Commodity Futures Trading Commission lacks authority to regulate the actual buying and selling of voluntary credits, it has published rules for trading derivatives—such as forwards and options—based on those credits.

In the end, government regulation may not be necessary because the inherent limitations of the market may circumscribe its own growth without external intervention. Additionality requires a financial subsidy. But if a company buys too many offset credits, the cumulative subsidies will lead to a damaging opportunity cost: the lost financial returns it could have generated with that much capital. The effect will be to reduce the company's financial performance. Shareholders, and the markets, will not be pleased.

There is a role for carbon offsets in the case of industries that cannot avoid a minimal level of carbon emissions, but this role will be modest if the additionality principle is respected.

In sum, the complexity and cost of carbon offsets makes it a poor tool to advance climate solutions. The best way to reduce carbon emissions is to reduce carbon emissions.

Climate Benchmarks: An Interesting Experiment

The European Union has set a standard for funds that intend to achieve the Paris objective of net-zero emissions by 2050. The key requirement is that the funds track indexes whose portfolios progressively decarbonize until the target is met.

The indexes, called "Paris-aligned benchmarks," are governed by three main rules, which came into effect in 2020. First, they screen out fossil fuels as well as some "sin" sectors like tobacco. Second, their "GHG intensity"—the ratio of carbon emissions to revenues (or sometimes a denominator based on market capitalization)—cannot be more than half that of a broad market index. Most importantly, this intensity score must decrease by 7 percent every year until it gets close to zero.

In principle, index managers could decrease the carbon intensity of their portfolio simply by buying more and more low-emitting stocks, like tech companies or retail trade, over time. But the rules preclude that by requiring that the sector weights of the indexes substantially equal those in a broad market index. This means that the index managers must select the cleanest companies in each sector—and must hope that these, or other companies in the sector, continue to get cleaner as the capital intensity ceiling drops lower every year.

To date, the climate funds have been able to meet the requirements primarily by the fossil fuel exclusion, which by itself lowers the portfolio capital intensity materially. Otherwise, the Paris-aligned funds look very similar to their broad market cousins.

Compare, for example, a Paris-aligned fund (SPDR MSCI ACWI Climate Paris Aligned ETF) to a large global market fund (iShares MSCI ACWI ETF).[19] The climate fund has scrubbed out energy, of course (with a concentration of only 0.02 percent), while the market fund has 4.37 percent of its portfolio in energy stocks. Still, nine of their top ten stock holdings are the same. Overall, their portfolio holdings overlap 96 percent.

The Paris-aligned benchmark is a clever concept, but Paris-aligned funds would need to command a large portion of the liquidity of the stock market to force companies down the carbon emissions curve. In that scenario, companies would frantically work to continuously cut emissions so they could earn a coveted place in their sector allocation in the index. But to date, although there are hundreds of Paris-aligned climate funds, their assets under management are a small fraction of the market total.

Most of the companies in the climate funds' portfolios are not on track to achieve net zero. This means that the universe of eligible stocks for the Paris-aligned indexes will continue to shrink as the decarbonization limit grows tighter, unless the broad economy weans itself off carbon. A day may come, not long in the future, when Paris-aligned index managers simply cannot find enough companies at low enough emission levels to make the math work.

18 Getting to Net Zero

Carbon emissions, as we have seen, will not be slashed by voluntarism or the interplay of supply and demand in the ordinary course. Only strong government action can check, and reverse, their rise.

There are signs of progress. In the United States, for example, GHG emissions had fallen 16 percent by 2022 from peak levels in 2007 (6.3 billion metric tons versus 7.5).[1] Notwithstanding the withdrawal of the United States from the Paris Agreement by the second Trump administration, a large part of that reduction is permanent, baked into the structure of the economy.

But the role of the state must increase materially if the planet is to avoid climate catastrophe. Globally, CO_2 emissions are continuing to climb, reaching a historic high in 2024, when 37.4 billion metric tons entered the atmosphere from burning fossil fuels.[2]

The negative effect of the US withdrawal from the Paris Agreement should not be overstated, as the Paris process is nothing but a talking shop, not a tool for concerted, decisive state action. The treaty commits its members collectively to limit temperate increase to 1.5 degrees Celsius above preindustrial levels, but the commitments are empty, as the treaty lacks compliance provisions and enforcement authority.

The good news is that each member country has submitted, through the Paris framework, a plan for GHG reduction, called a Nationally Determined Contribution. In the aggregate, the NDCs envision cutting global GHG emissions by 88 percent during the course of the twenty-first century. The bad news is that only 10 percent of this planned reduction has been enacted in domestic legislation, and only 0.4 percent has actually happened so far. Additionally, more than 90 percent of the reductions are not planned to take place until after 2040, when most current leaders will be long gone.[3]

The Paris mechanism helps to shine a light on the state of the climate and on what nations are doing—or not doing—to ease the crisis, but ultimately countries will take climate action only to the extent that they determine, as sovereign entities, that it accords with their national interest. The biggest players—China, India, the United States, and the European Union, which collectively account for half of global emissions[4]—have the greatest role to play. Their GHG emissions are large enough to affect the climate directly, including in their own countries, and their economies have global reach. Smaller nations, consistent with their role in geopolitics generally, will need to make alliances, use moral suasion, and adroitly apply their limited influence on the global stage to have some say on climate strategies.

Although the science of climate change is intricate and complicated, its core message is simple: fossil fuel combustion is chiefly to blame. And the largest part of the solution is even simpler: electricity.

Burning coal, oil, and natural gas accounts for 93 percent of CO_2 emissions and 68 percent of total GHG emissions.[5] But in the industrialized countries that produce the bulk of these emissions, fossil fuel use is heavily concentrated in only three areas: generating electricity for the grid, running vehicles, and producing on-site energy for power-intensive industries like steel mills.

In the United States, for example, 92 percent of coal is used for electricity and the remainder is used in industrial plants. Sixty-six percent of oil is used for gasoline and other transportation needs, 6 percent for electricity, and 28 percent for other purposes including feedstock for plastics. Natural gas is used mainly for industry (32 percent) and electricity (38 percent), but a significant portion goes to residences and commercial buildings for heating, power, and cooking (26 percent).[6]

The alternatives are obvious and all revolve around electricity: utility-scale solar and wind projects, vehicles that run on batteries, and an enlarged grid to supply heavy industry. These are huge undertakings, of course, but they are clearly understood, the technology to achieve them is largely in hand, and their accomplishment would bring us near the goal of rescuing the planet.

Building a political consensus for the electricity transition will require an immense effort, starting at the grass-roots level, but corporations resistant to change, as well as well-meaning but misguided special interest groups, may distract our attention and cloud our judgment.

Take forestry, for example. Trees are a crucial component of the carbon cycle, of course, but scaling reforestation up to meaningful levels of incremental CO_2 reduction is a pipe dream. Shaving 0.15 degrees Celsius off global warming would require planting one trillion new trees on an area three times the size of India. Even this is an optimistic estimate, without accounting for the rising mortality rate of forests from drought, wildfires, and disease, stimulated by temperature rise.[7]

Tech billionaire and philanthropist Bill Gates was asked if planting trees could help save the planet. His reply should guide our thinking generally: "That's complete nonsense. I mean, are we the science people or the idiots? Which one do we want to be?"[8] Recycling, moving your thermostat up a degree or two in the summer, taking the train instead of an airplane—these things may make us feel better about ourselves, but they do nothing substantial to solve the climate crisis.

But while the path forward is clear, it is not smooth. Fortunately, it is now cheaper to build and operate solar and wind power plants than ones running on coal, oil, or gas,[9] but replacing the existing fleet of fossil-fuel-fired power plants by renewable utilities will be a massive project.

Moreover, generating electricity cleanly is pointless if the power cannot flow to where it is needed. Building out an extensive network of vehicle charging stations, and expanding the grid to accommodate the high power demands of manufacturing, will take not only vast amounts of capital but also complicated permitting procedures for infrastructure improvement like high-capacity transmission lines.

Governments that commit to the electricity transition will need to back up their ambitions with funding. Currently, global capital spending on climate change runs about $1.2 trillion annually, about evenly split between the public and private sectors. Moving to net zero by 2050 is estimated to raise those costs sevenfold, to about $8–$10 trillion annually, well over $200 trillion in total.[10]

Countries have two main ways to finance climate projects: tax credits and direct expenditure. Take the example of the Inflation Reduction Act (IRA) in the United States, the flagship accomplishment of the Biden administration's climate program. The second Trump administration came into office committed to overturn the law or gut its implementation, but, as enacted, it stood as a case study in comprehensive government climate policy.

When the bill passed in 2022, researchers estimated that it would result in almost $400 billion of incremental government support of climate action. By itself, the IRA was projected to reduce America's GHG emissions by 8–17 percent.[11]

The spending was estimated to be divided between $271 billion of tax credits and direct expenditures of $121 billion. Take the larger component, tax credits, first.

Tax credits are direct reductions in tax bills. They cut tax expense dollar for dollar, as opposed to tax-deductible expenses, which have only a fractional effect on tax payable. The largest tax credit allowance in the IRA, estimated at $131 billion, was in the form of a new credit of $5 per megawatt hour for wind and solar power investment and production. The credits were tantamount to cash, as in many cases recipients could sell unused tax credits.

Tax credits have a long history of being granted to defray research and development costs and to shelter infant industries. Among others, they have been instrumental in the growth and maturation of solar and wind power. For example, even before the passage of the IRA, the giant conglomerate Berkshire Hathaway invested about $30 billion in wind turbines and infrastructure in Iowa, seeking to make the state "the wind capital of the world, the Saudi Arabia of wind." The company's long-term chair, Warren Buffett, revered for his strong capitalist values and business acumen, said government support was the determining factor in the strategy: "We wouldn't do [it] without the production tax credit we get."[12]

Buffett added that he had no intention of closing the company's existing coal power plants despite their heavy pollution—unless the government changed the rules.

> If people want us to junk our coal plants, either our shareholders or the consumer is going to pay for it. You can argue that unfortunately the consumer pays for it, but then the trouble is they pay for it if they happen to live in the place where a utility has 50 per cent [of their energy] coming from coal. If they happen to be in some other territory, they don't pay for it. So, there's a cost to somebody . . . the question is how it gets absorbed, but overwhelmingly that has to be a governmental activity. . . . *The government has to play the part of modifying a market system.*[13]

The second bucket of IRA funding was direct expenditure for a variety of clean purposes, including forest conservation and industrial decarbonization. This included $27 billion for the Greenhouse Gas Reduction Fund, much of which was targeted to specialized community development lenders in the form of grants, equity capital, or loan guarantees—blended finance, as discussed in chapter 14.

The EPA estimated that this government funding would catalyze nearly seven times as much private investment.[14] A study by the consulting firm McKinsey gave an even higher estimate: twelve times.[15]

Pricing Carbon

But government financing alone, even if leveraged, will not be sufficient to wean the world economy from its dependence on fossil fuel. The negative externalities of GHG emissions are too costly for governments to bear solo. The logical answer is to internalize the externality—to put a price on carbon so that its expense can be reflected in business like that of any other input.

The bellwether for this policy is Sweden, which began taxing carbon in 1991 at $22 per ton and gradually increased the price until it reached $119 in 2023.[16] The result was a 33 percent decrease in carbon emissions.

Sweden is cold in the winter, but fossil fuel use in heating has dropped by more than 90 percent, replaced by heat pumps, wood pellets, and burning waste. The country aims to achieve net zero by 2045, before the 2050 global target.

In Sweden's case, "modifying a market system," in Buffett's phrase, apparently has benefited the economy rather than holding it back. The country's annual GDP growth has averaged 2.2 percent since it began taxing carbon, slightly higher than its average growth rate in the twenty previous years (2.1 percent). Compared to the European Union as a whole, Sweden's average growth rate lagged by 0.8 percent from 1971 to 1990, but since then it has exceeded its peers by 0.4 percent.[17]

Looking more broadly, an analysis of fifteen countries with carbon taxes concluded that there was no statistically significant evidence that these taxes had impacted either GDP or employment growth, positively or negatively.[18]

But taxing carbon can be politically problematic, and few countries have gone as far as Sweden. The median carbon tax per ton among twenty-two countries that tax carbon is $31.[19] This is below the estimate in a widely cited review that $40–$80 would be the range necessary to keep global warming at 2 degrees Celsius or below, rising to $50–$100 per ton by 2030.[20]

A better way to squeeze carbon out of the economy than directly taxing it is to ration it and let the market determine the price. This principle has been embodied in numerous government-mandated "emissions trading systems" (ETS), also known as "cap and trade."

About a quarter of global emissions is now subject to cap and trade, up from only 5 percent in 2010. Some variant of cap and trade is operating in forty-nine countries and regions, including some parts of the United States, the European Union, and China.[21]

In a prototypical ETS, the government sets an overall limit on emissions from polluting industries, such as fossil-fuel-fired power plants, and then auctions off permits to pollute. Over time, the state lowers the limit, so permits become scarcer and their prices rise. To afford the ever-costlier permits, emitters have three choices: raise their prices, become more efficient, or transition to renewables. The government uses the funds raised from permit sales, either for general purposes or for climate-related activities.

Gradually, the net is spread to other industries, like manufacturing and aviation. A secondary market in permits—in which those who need more buy from those who have an excess—helps to ensure that prices reflect the true economic cost of carbon.

Cap and trade functions very well in a closed market, but in open economies there is a risk of cheaply priced imports, made in areas with weak or nonexistent carbon price controls, undercutting domestic manufacturers. To counter this, carbon markets like the European Union's are implementing adjustment mechanisms—akin to tariffs—so that carbon used in imported goods is effectively priced the same as in the importer's economy.

Some cap-and-trade systems allow the trading of voluntary carbon credits (which we looked at in the previous chapter) alongside the mandatory credits (also called compliance credits) that are an inherent part of the ETS program. The advantage is that these voluntary credits are generally higher quality than the ones in private markets, as they are vetted and approved by regulators, or agencies delegated by regulators. The disadvantage is that if they are too numerous, voluntary credits may bring down the overall secondary market price, including the price of compliance credits, as they are economically equivalent—each typically carries the right to emit one ton of CO_2. The rationale of an ETS is to make carbon more expensive over time so that polluters will eventually abandon the practice. An influx of voluntary credits could undermine the process.

To complicate the picture further, some countries explicitly allow carbon credits to be sold by renewable power producers, with no evidence of additionality, in order to provide a nongovernmental subsidy to the industry.

In the United States, "renewable energy credits" (or "certificates"), mainly under state regulation, are a $13 billion a year industry.[22] Companies that buy RECs claim Scope 2 emissions reductions, but these are phantom cuts.

The literature is mixed on the economic impact of cap and trade. Like a direct tax, rationing and auctioning carbon transfers money from business to government and, at some level, slows the economy, assuming that the government's spending of the additional revenue does not have an equivalent level of economic stimulus.

But by forcing the pace of the economy's transition away from carbon, cap and trade whittles down the costs of the negative externalities imposed by fossil fuels on the world at large. And by locating these costs at the level of the companies where they arise, an ETS put the interests of the companies and society in alignment instead of at cross-purposes.

The empirical evidence shows that the economic damage from cap and trade, if any, seems slight. In some instances, it seems to go the other way. For example, in the United States, in 2008–2021, the nine northeastern states in the Regional Greenhouse Gas Initiative, a cap-and-trade program for power plants, had 13 percent higher growth per capita than the rest of the country, even while their power sector CO_2 emissions fell 10 percent more.[23]

Several other parts of the United States also have cap-and-trade programs. The largest, in California, covers about 85 percent of the state's emissions, has reduced carbon emissions below 1990 levels, and is on track to reduce emissions by 80 percent by 2050. With carbon capture and storage to account for the remaining emissions, the state's policy is to achieve net zero by 2045.[24]

But in the country overall, support for ETS remains soft. On an ideological basis, conservatives oppose cap and trade as a tax increase and an unwarranted government intrusion into the operation of free markets. And companies, especially in the fossil fuel sector, are in no hurry to assume costs that are now being freely transferred to the world at large.

Opponents point out, validly, that electricity prices at the meter often increase when utilities are subject to cap and trade, as power companies are typically regulated entities and can pass the permit costs directly to their customers. But proponents counter that consumers get value for money in the form of cleaner air and less climate change. However, it's difficult to assign a dollar value to these benefits, whereas higher power bills are a direct and tangible hit to the pocketbook.

Conclusion: Where Do We Go from Here?

What have we learned so far? In sum, corporations are not voluntary change agents; screening out stocks doesn't alter company behavior; social shareholders can't get seats at the table; ESG doesn't boost social performance; impact investing does this but at the cost of financial returns; and only strong government action can save the world from burning up, but governments are far behind the curve.

Isn't there any good news? Well, yes. Although the path forward leads steeply uphill, some helpful steps are being taken. For example, some cap-and-trade systems, like the European Union's ETS, are successfully playing a critical role in managing the transition of large economies to net zero without disruption. Also, we are seeing innovative efforts, like the invention of "benefit corporations," to try to make corporate governance more responsive to social concerns, as we discuss later. Even the anti-woke campaign does a useful service—although coming from the wrong direction—in reminding us that finance and business cannot substitute for government in strengthening the social safety net and protecting the environment.

Making progress depends on clear vision and undistracted attention. If we presume that listed companies will exercise great social responsibility, despite answering to an unforgiving market, we only encourage them to put on a show of virtue, masking their primordial objective to maximize profits. Asking a corporation to do a "social audit" is not asking a lot (even though social shareholders rarely succeed in getting these resolutions passed at AGMs). But asking it to kindly cut earnings in order to implement pay equity, or to enter the uncertain world of a climate transition while their current business model reliably churns out profits, is pointless.

It follows that, as investors, we should refuse to join the charade of ESG and let those who manage our money know our feelings. ESG funds are market funds in fancy clothes—we should stop paying extra fees for the finery. But the biggest benefit we will gain from sweeping away ESG is confronting the sobering reality that social and environmental progress carries a cost and takes sustained effort. Like every confidence game, ESG only succeeds when the mark believes that he is beating the odds. Time to leave the table.

Steering corporations toward more socially positive behavior doesn't mean sacrificing the prodigious capacity of capitalism to create wealth. But as we have seen before, the right mechanism for this is legislation and regulation, not ethical investment and moral suasion.

Just as the Progressives and the New Dealers attacked the inequities of their own time with legislative initiatives, we need to end the shocking return of Gilded Age inequality in the twenty-first century by updating and strengthening supervision over the corporate sector and finance industry. This may seem even more daunting after the arrival of Donald Trump in the White House for the second time, but it may just mean the backlash, when it comes, will be even stronger.

As we saw in the previous chapter, governments can mitigate climate change with a combination of financial incentives and, most important, a mandatory system that treats carbon like any other cost of doing business. Here are some other key issues that we need to deal with through the political process.

Restoring the Role of Labor

Making corporations more socially responsible starts with restoring the power triangle that provided stability and an equitable balance during the Golden Age of Capitalism. When organized labor wins, so do we all, as union agreements set standards for nonunionized companies as well, and unions are responsive to the needs of lower-income and less-advantaged populations.

Much of the union decline in the United States has come from economic forces beyond government control. Manufacturing has lost workforce share relative to service industries. Service workers are harder to organize, as their jobs are more dispersed and more varied, and a sense of solidarity more challenging to build and maintain. In addition, as global trade has burgeoned, an influx of relatively cheap imports, both goods and services, has suppressed wage growth throughout the lower levels of the economy and undermined unions' bargaining strength.

But state governments have accelerated the slide by implementing "right-to-work" laws forbidding "closed shops" where union membership is a prerequisite of employment. On their face, the laws, in effect in twenty-seven states, appear in line with a worker's freedom to choose. But they give rise to the "free rider" quandary, where a nonunion worker, who does not pay fees to the union, receives the benefit of agreements negotiated with the union, as they apply to all in the workplace. Free riders sap union membership and bargaining power, and make it easier for companies to keep unions out. The presence of a union typically generates returns to workers far in excess of the fees they pay. But in states with right-to-work laws, where unions have been weakened, workers earn less, have worse health and retirement benefits, and die at higher rates from workplace accidents than their counterparts in states without these laws.[1]

Legislation creating a nationwide "right to organize" has been introduced in Congress on several occasions but has failed to pass. We need it to become a reality, together with updating other labor union protections to reflect the circumstances of the current economy and workplace.

At the same time, the role of the National Labor Relations board should be expanded, and its independence from partisan politics strengthened. This powerful federal agency is charged with enforcing union legal rights and its decisions set the tone for management-labor relations.

The five NLRB commissioners are appointed by the president to serve five-year staggered terms, with one rolling off every year. This selection process gives presidents wide latitude to shape the board in their image over time. For example, the NLRB ordered the reinstatement of more illegally fired workers in the first year after the election of Joe Biden, a prolabor president, than in all four years of the preceding Donald Trump administration.[2] But when Trump again took office in 2025, he attempted to circumvent even the limited bipartisan nature of the board by firing—without cause, in apparent violation of the agency's statute[3]—a Democratic member of the board whose term was still valid.

Such hyperpartisan maneuvering needs to be precluded by updating the NLRB's charter and giving it the resources and independence it needs to ensure a level balance of power between employer and employee. Most important, the board should include one or more seats for representatives chosen by, and directly accountable to, workers, not the executive branch.

The declining force of organized labor has repercussions throughout the economy. Abusive "gig" employment, a fall in the real value of the minimum wage, and a weakened Occupational Safety and Health Administration[4] are just a few symptoms of the current power imbalance.

Organized labor typically stands against corporate concentration, but as labor has fragmented in recent decades, while governments have held antitrust regulations in abeyance, concentration has increased dramatically. This has affected more than three-fourths of American industries, as we saw in chapter 5.

The harm to all stakeholders from corporate concentration, not just workers, is widespread. When companies increase their market power, their profit margins rise, but their workers' wages stagnate, growth slows, productivity falls, income inequality deepens, regulators retreat, and large-scale lobbying buys political influence to keep the merry-go-round turning.[5]

The equilibrium among labor, business, and government that prevailed prior to the neoliberal ascendancy cannot be reestablished until voters mobilize to elect lawmakers who respect the rights of labor, promote the vital role of unions in creating a more just and equitable society, and unwind the ever-tightening spiral of corporate concentration.

Busting the Modern "Money Trust"

One of the most concentrated industries in the country, as well as a prime mover of harmful concentration across the economy, is asset management. The "Big Three" asset managers—BlackRock, Vanguard, and State Street—account for about one-third of the total market ($19.1 trillion of $61.5 trillion)[6] and, collectively, are the largest owners of 88 percent of the S&P 500,[7] including fourteen of the fifteen largest banks (State Street itself is one of them).[8] Moreover, Vanguard is the largest owner of BlackRock and State Street, and those two hold large shares in each other.[9] Below these giants are a number of lesser, but still disproportionately large, players.

The breadth of these managers' holdings, and their incestuous relationships, recall the "Money Trust" of the late nineteenth century. This was a small group of investment banks, led by the notorious finance mogul J.P. Morgan, whose predominance over a vast swath of industries through mutual share ownership and interlocking directorships stifled competition and led an alarmed Congress to create the Federal Reserve banking system. Today, beneficial share ownership is widely dispersed, but asset managers acting as agents for end-owners exercise as much control over capital flows as their Gilded Age counterparts.

Large asset managers not only control the largest blocks of voting shares directly but often set the course for many institutional investors to follow. However, these titans face breathtaking conflicts of interest.

For one, they often run both equity funds and bond funds, leveraging—literally—their corporate governance influence, as they could in principle withhold debt investment from companies whose equity strategies they disagree with.[10]

In addition, they frequently seek to manage the pension funds and internal liquidity of the same companies whose stocks they hold in their portfolios. Financial assets on the balance sheets of corporations comprise a large portion of the overall market. Clearly, fund managers cannot afford to antagonize executives of companies they are pursuing as clients by disagreeing with them in the boardroom.

Moreover, most of the shares that the leading managers hold are bundled into passive funds,[11] which are tightly tied to market indexes, without the possibility of meaningful discretion. And even the funds they actively manage typically hew closely to their benchmarks.

The result is that the biggest asset managers are muscle-bound giants. They cannot divest large capitalization stocks from their portfolios without inflating their tracking error. They dare not vote their proxies against the wishes of firms whose assets they manage, or propose to manage. They stand by, or lend support, while large companies tamp down threats from smaller, more dynamic players, leading to a continuous rise in competition-killing concentration across all sectors. And, as we have seen, they leave social shareholders, with their gently worded pleas to show more concern about E&S issues, at the gate.

Their conflicts of interest make the large asset managers intrinsically faulty stewards of corporate governance. They should be relieved of their voting privileges so that shareholders can directly decide how to cast their proxies at AGMs. Criticism from both left and right has led the biggest players to take initial steps in this direction, called "pass-through voting," but the journey has just begun.

BlackRock, for example, allows its institutional clients in index funds three options: leave the proxies with BlackRock, give them to a selected list of proxy advisors, or create a custom voting policy. However, about 77 percent of eligible clients take the default, BlackRock control, instead of assuming some responsibility for shareholder voting, even though they could easily choose, in the second option, from a proxy advisor menu including a variety of clearly-articulated strategies, from "Wealth" to "Climate," "ESG," and "Sustainability."[12]

The reluctance of institutional clients—like pension funds, insurance companies, and banks—to go into the program may be due in part to its novelty, as well as its complexity and cost, in particular the customization option. But probably more significant is that many institutions are as risk-averse as the asset managers themselves, and might fear blowback from either anti-woke conservatives or climate-aware liberals if they commit to certain voting policies.

Not taking a stand, they may believe, is the safest course. But of course, not taking a stand *is* taking a stand—in favor of the status quo and against change.

The litmus test of pass-through voting will be if and when it is rolled out to retail investors. The Big Three have all conducted pilot projects. However, the asset managers may be hesitant to commit themselves to work through the complicated legal, regulatory, and administrative issues inherent in enlarging the programs to encompass many millions of people, often holding their shares through several levels of intermediaries, like brokers, personal advisors, and 401(k)s. More importantly, the managers may not like the results if their retail clients are more willing than they are to vote against portfolio companies' management.

But this is precisely why pass-through voting, for retail as well as institutional clients, should be made mandatory, especially in index funds. In actively managed funds, an argument can be made that asset managers need more leeway, as their goal is to create alpha, not match an index exactly. They need to take views on strategic issues and back them up with votes. But even in an active fund, the asset manager should engage with those whose money it manages, not just portfolio companies, to ensure they are faithfully representing their views.

In passive funds, however, where the managers mechanically mirror indexes, there is no justification whatsoever for managers to have control over proxies. Their role is ministerial, and their views on AGM matters are irrelevant to their work. Voting authority should lie with shareholders only, not accrue to managers to use to advance their own ends.

Pass-through voting addresses one of the two root problems of a capitalist economy dominated by asset management, known as "control-based power." But it leaves intact the other, "exit-based power."[13] Asset managers who are too large, too conflicted, or both, to freely exercise the ability to divest shares are fundamentally deficient. They continually reinforce the market power of the large capitalization companies that sit at the top of their portfolios and are treasured clients on the side. The only way to dissolve this mutually reinforcing, but harmful, relationship is to break up the behemoths.

First, index funds should be separated and managed by specialist agencies that continually strive to perfect the technical processes of replicating benchmarks, driving down transaction costs and ensuring transparency and efficiency—and implementing proxy instructions from clients. This is "management" only in a narrow, mechanical sense. The function of a hands-off passive fund operator is intrinsically different from—and in conflict with—that of an active manager, whose job is to capitalize on mispriced stocks, anticipating or even triggering valuation changes that could alter companies' positions in the index, perhaps even the index performance overall.

Second, asset managers should not be allowed to leverage their corporate governance power by managing funds that could invest in both the equity and the debt of the same portfolio company. Separating the two asset classes also recognizes that the interests of creditors and shareholders are distinct, and may diverge in some cases. Even though the managers today employ separate teams for each asset class, there should be no possibility of temptation to let the intentions of one bleed into the other.

Third, and most important, asset managers should be small and agile, not huge and sluggish. And they should be barred from managing the assets of the companies whose shares they hold. This would let competition flourish instead of a small cartel sharing the market among themselves.

In an industry with myriad smaller players, each seeking to distinguish its offerings from competitors, investors would have a widespread array of choices. For example, some fund managers would specialize in the hunt for new, innovative enterprises that challenge the stale preeminence of established leaders, instead of helping to tighten further the straitjacket of corporate concentration. Some managers would predicate their business model on offering a longer-term view of stakeholder value than is the norm today, committing to prove that certain social and economic actions should be taken now, even if their payoff takes some time, as the returns will justify the wait. Without conflicting loyalties, managers in this more nimble, decentralized industry would not hesitate to challenge the firms whose shares they held on behalf of clients.

Finally, and critically, a deconcentrated fund management industry would be shorn of the vast influence it now exercises over elected officials to block progress toward greater social responsibility in the corporate and financial communities.

Reforming Private Equity

As we saw in chapter 14, mainstream PE leaves social concerns behind in its rapacious drive for investment returns. While our focus in the chapter was on the threat that PE poses to impact investing in developing countries, remedying PE's flaws would benefit industrialized countries even more, as that is where the bulk of its $10 trillion assets under management is concentrated.

Bills have been introduced in Congress several times to curb PE's excesses, with support from many Democratic legislators, unions, and social interest groups, but have failed to pass. The October 2024 "Stop Wall Street Looting Act" was a good example of the kinds of guardrails that need to be put in place. Among its provisions were the following:

- *Accountability:* The act would make PE firms responsible for the debts of their portfolio companies so that they could not evade the consequences of deliberately bankrupting them. In the event of bankruptcy, it would give higher priority to workers' severance and pension claims and bar outsized payments to executives.
- *Capital adequacy:* PE owners could not take out equity capital from a portfolio company for at least four years after its acquisition. For two years after that, they could not weaken the company's capital base by withdrawing an amount greater than 10 percent of the company's debt.

In addition, PE managers would be penalized for loading unsustainable debt onto companies they own, by taking away the tax deductibility of interest paid on excessive debt with respect to the equity base.

- *Unwarranted fees:* The act would end PE owners' ability to extract spurious "monitoring" or "advisory" fees from owned companies. Portfolio companies could retain the cash to improve the business.

Increasing Funding and Investor Access in Impact

Governments should not only immunize impact investing against unscrupulous PE funds, they should materially increase their support overall for this sector. A dollar of official impact finance can catalyze many more when embodied in "blended" structures, as we saw earlier. Government development agencies need to stop competing with private sector finance through insistence on market rates and start measuring their effectiveness in terms of social and environmental objectives achieved.

Moreover, in developing countries impactful companies spread benefits beyond their immediate stakeholder communities. Successful businesses serve as training grounds and mentors for future entrepreneurs and senior managers. Companies with positive corporate cultures set standards for their peers. Impact investments can help develop and strengthen the entire infrastructure of business in emerging nations, and this in turn leads to progress in other key state functions like the rule of law and competent, honest regulation.

As well as investing directly, governments can also play a critical role in marshaling private sector support for impact finance by helping develop investment vehicles that are accessible to retail investors and more attractive to institutional investors than their current options. The risky and illiquid nature of most impact investments hinders their packaging into listed liquid funds like mutual funds and ETFs, thus substantially reducing the potential universe of investors. But governments and regulators can address these issues with tools like partial guarantees, standby liquidity facilities, and "last resort" asset purchase funds. We won't know to what extent investors will accept the social-financial trade-off implicit in impact investing until we remove the systemic barriers that keep them from being able to make the choice.

Writing Social Goals into Charters

In recent years, a number of states have established a new legal form of corporation, the public benefit corporation (PBC), that contains in its charter a commitment to social or environmental goals. The boards of directors of PBCs are legally required to "balance"—the term used by the Delaware statute, the model for most PBC legislation—two distinct concerns: profit maximization and social goals as articulated in the charter.

More than ten thousand companies in the United States have chosen this corporate form, including fifteen that are publicly listed.[14] But that is a small fraction of the corporate community, and empirical evidence so far is scant on the relative social and financial performance of PBCs versus traditional corporations.

PBCs have to weigh social good produced, or social harm precluded, against any reduction in profits. For example, a clothing company committed to soil preservation might decide to pay a bit more for organically produced cotton. Or a manufacturer with community relations in its charter might sponsor training centers, museums, and medical clinics. But quantifying social value and comparing it to financial returns is a complicated exercise, in which subjectivity and unverifiable assumptions are hard to avoid. And how much is too much?

As a check on the balance between financial and social concerns, shareholders can sue if they feel the company is leaning too far in one direction. But that right is denied to third parties whose interests the social charter provisions are ostensibly there to protect. Even PBCs put shareholders on the highest rung of the ladder of corporate purpose.

Nevertheless, even if stakeholders had legal standing, the biggest flaw of PBCs would remain: Their social goals are so vaguely expressed that they cannot serve as a good guide for board decisions, nor can they provide a solid legal basis for holding the company accountable.[15]

For example, eyeglass company Warby Parker states in its charter that its public benefit is "to provide access to products and services that promote vision and eye health and to work towards positively impacting the communities in which the corporation operates."[16]

The company gives away a pair of glasses in an underserved community for every one it sells, but if it stopped doing this, would that be a violation of its charter? Also, although it is generally well-regarded socially, it only receives a two out of five rating, "Not Good Enough," from Good on You, the nonprofit ethical fashion rating organization,[17] mainly because it does not disclose its action, or lack, with respect to many important E&S issues. But even if Warby ran sweatshops and dumped chemicals into the water, would free glasses be "positively impacting" enough to ward off liability for breaching the charter?

Legislation to make PBCs the norm would have the positive effect of making companies think harder about their roles. It would elevate the importance of social issues at the board and throughout the company. But it would still run up against the reluctance of companies to define charter commitments sufficiently to create an actionable legal liability.

Even companies that approached the topic in good faith would find it challenging. Like a fractal, the closer you look at social issues, the more complexity you see. Terms that are clearly defined now will seem quaint and obsolete later. Quantitative standards that make sense in the current environment will soon become outmoded.

Giving legal standing to stakeholders alongside shareholders would only heighten the risk to directors and company executives and push them harder to adopt statements of meaningless generality.

In sum, the PBC can draw attention to social concerns and help companies to focus on their role in the community. It can give owners, especially those of private corporations, an effective means to express and channel preexisting altruistic impulses. But it cannot by itself implant social responsibility in a company that doesn't already have it in their DNA.

As a sidebar, it is important not to confuse a "public benefit corporation"—or "benefit corporation," as some statutes term it—with a "B Corporation," which, confusingly, is also sometimes referred to as a "benefit corporation."

A "B Corporation," or "B Corp," is a company that has received a certification, widely known and usually well respected, from a private, nonprofit rating agency, called B Lab. Companies applying for the designation go through a lengthy assessment covering five areas: governance, workers, community, environment, and customers. B Corporations also are required to post extensive disclosure statements on the B Lab website annually. There are more than eight thousand B Corporations in more than ninety countries, including well-known brands such as Ben & Jerry's ice cream, sports retailer Patagonia (see chapter 14), and Natura, the owner of Body Shop.

Many praise B Corporations for signing up to adhere to a rigorous set of social standards. "The B Corp movement is one of the most important of our lifetime, built on the simple fact that business impacts and serves more than just shareholders—it has an equal responsibility to the community and to the planet," said a former Patagonia CEO.[18]

But many charge that the program does not go far enough. "Any company can become a B Corp," said the former chief executive of the World Fair Trade Organization. "It is its biggest strength, but also its biggest weakness."[19]

In 2022, for example, the coffee machine maker Nespresso became a B Corporation, appalling many in the B Corp community who protested in an open letter to B Lab that "the B Corp standard is at risk."[20] They said: "Nespresso's abysmal track record on human rights from child labor and wage theft to abuse of factory workers is well documented. . . . Nespresso's extractive business model is publicly known to be fundamentally at odds with the ethical and just future B Corps want to build and should have structurally been a barrier to Nespresso's B Corp Certification."

Despite the outrage, Nespresso was allowed to retain its B Corp status. According to the B Lab website, "Nestlé Nespresso SA is the pioneer and reference for highest-quality portioned coffee."[21]

B Lab continually updates its standards, but the requirements will remain relatively loose so long as the B Corp program aims for a large, global membership. The risk will persist that companies achieve a passing score and are awarded the B Corp banner while failing to clear the bar on material social or environmental issues.

Making Boards More Accountable

Social responsibility cannot be built into the nature of a corporate form, but it can be established top-down on a case-by-case basis by the directors who bear the ultimate authority. Most people assume that directors have a fiduciary obligation to maximize shareholder value. But while that is common practice, it is not a legal requirement. Put simply, under the well-established business judgment rule, directors have a fiduciary responsibility to govern in the best interests of the *companies* on whose boards they sit, even if their decisions do not result in the highest level of financial gains for *shareholders*.

As Cornell Law School Professor Lynn Stout, who wrote a well-regarded book on the subject, put it, "As long as [directors] do not take [company] assets for themselves, they can give them to charity; spend them on raises and health care for employees; refuse to pay dividends so as to build up a cash cushion that benefits creditors; and pursue low-profit projects that benefit the community, society or the environment. They can do all these things even if the result is to decrease—not increase—shareholder value."[22]

Of course, most directors do their utmost to maximize value for shareholders, for a simple reason: They want to keep shareholders electing them. Moreover, most directors at large corporations receive most of their pay in the form of shares or equity-linked instruments like warrants or options.[23] If they adopt social policies that reduce profits, they are taking money out of their own pockets.

Directors are human. They cannot impartially weigh the benefit of social policies when doing so harms their own interests. To remove this conflict, directors should receive fixed compensation. It is not a question of paying for talent. Directors at S&P 500 companies typically earn over $300,000 per year.[24] That would be a handsome salary, even if two-thirds were not in stock. Besides, most of them earn twice that, or more, since 66 percent of them sit on more than one board.[25]

The current size of the pay package is sufficient to attract the highest-quality candidates for board seats. There is no need to include equity upside in the envelope, as it lands directors squarely in an unmanageable conflict of interest and prejudices their consideration of social and environmental issues.

Another simple but powerful reform is to mandate worker representation on boards. The example of Germany shows the beneficial effects, not just for labor but for the overall company. In Germany, companies with less than 500 employees can choose to have their staff elect one-third of the supervisory board or to forego labor representation. A study showed that companies that opted for worker representation on the board had more women directors and did better financially. Pay was slightly higher, but the companies could easily afford it as fixed assets per employee and capital stocks were significantly higher.[26] The relationship between labor and capital is not zero-sum after all.

Another study found that electing an even larger proportion of worker representatives, 50 percent, led to a greater likelihood that companies would set specific emissions reduction targets and disclose comprehensive information on their social performance.[27]

In principle, allocating director seats to other types of stakeholders would also improve governance, but deciding how to nominate these directors—who represents the climate?—would not be straightforward. Government should set the rules for corporate governance, but not make the decisions—politics must remain out of the director selection process.

These two measures—making directors economically impartial and allocating a fair share of board seats to workers representatives—would help free corporate governance from the customary, but not legally required, stranglehold of shareholder value over larger company purpose.

Answering the Mill Girl's Call

Asset managers who are not in thrall to large capitalization stocks and who eagerly seek to invest in innovative, dynamic companies. Corporate directors who look beyond quarterly earnings reports and are unafraid to commit companies to socially responsible policies, even if the payoff takes time. Revitalized labor unions that restore balance in the workplace and help rebuild the hollowed-out middle class. Carbon priced like any other input so businesses can adapt while the world steps back from the precipice of global warming.

These things can happen in a democracy. What may seem politically infeasible today will become a reality if we remain active and focused—if we keep reminding ourselves that the great reforms of earlier eras also seemed unthinkable until they became inevitable.

Across two centuries, the plaintive challenge of a mill girl is as fresh and important today as it has ever been. We must keep faith with Harriet Robinson and all that she stands for. We must mix a little conscience with our capital.

Notes

Introduction

1. Global Sustainable Investment Alliance, *Global Sustainable Investment Review 2022* (Global Sustainable Investment Alliance, 2023), https://www.gsi-alliance.org/wp-content/uploads/2023/12/GSIA-Report-2022.pdf.

2. "Investors Say They Can Change the World, if They Only Knew How: Six Things to Know About ESG and Retail Investors," FINRA, March 2022, https://www.finrafoundation.org/sites/finrafoundation/files/Consumer-Insights-Money-and-Investing.pdf.

3. Polly Bindman, "Why ESG Funds Are Full of Fossil Fuels," Energy Monitor, April 28, 2023, https://www.energymonitor.ai/finance/sustainable-finance/why-esg-funds-are-full-of-fossil-fuels-but-thats-okay/.

4. Gong Cheng et al., "Sovereign Green Bonds: A Catalyst for Sustainable Debt Market Development?," Working Paper No. 24/120 (International Monetary Fund, June 2024), https://www.imf.org/-/media/Files/Publications/WP/2024/English/wpiea2024120-print-pdf.ashx.

5. Global Impact Investing Network, *2022: Sizing the Impact Investing Market* (Global Impact Investing Network, 2022), https://thegiin.org/publication/research/impact-investing-market-size-2022/.

6. Jeremy Salvucci, "Institutional Investors: Who They Are & What They Do," TheStreet, April 8, 2024, https://www.thestreet.com/dictionary/institutional-investors.

7. Zhi Da and Mitch Warachka, "The Disparity Between Long-Term and Short-Term Forecasted Earnings Growth," *Journal of Financial Economics* 100, no. 2 (2011): 424–442, https://doi.org/10.1016/j.jfineco.2010.10.015.

8. We explore this more fully in chapter 6.

9. See chapter 5.

10. Jonathan M. V. Davis and Bhashkar Mazumder, "The Decline in Intergenerational Mobility After 1980," Stone Center on Socio-Economic Inequality, February 2020, https://stonecenter.gc.cuny.edu/research/the-decline-in-intergenerational-mobility-after-1980/.

Chapter 1

1. Edward Pessen, "Chapter 2: Builders of the Young Republic," *History*, US Department of Labor, https://www.dol.gov/general/aboutdol/history/chapter2.

2. The Lowell System and the milieu of the "mill girls" are well documented. Sources consulted for this chapter include Philip S. Foner, ed., *The Factory Girls* (University of Illinois Press, 1977); Thomas Dublin, *Women at Work* (Columbia University Press, 1979); Norman Ware, *The Industrial Worker 1840–1860* (Quadrangle Books, 1964); David E. Shi, *The Simple Life* (Oxford University Press, 1985), chap. 4; Robert F. Dalzell Jr., *Enterprising Elite* (Harvard University Press, 1987).

3. Massachusetts Bureau of Statistics of Labor, *Fourteenth Annual Report* (Massachusetts Bureau of Statistics of Labor, 1883), 384.

4. Massachusetts Bureau of Statistics of Labor, *Fourteenth Annual Report*, 384.

5. Shaun Steven Nichols, "Crisis Capital: Industrial Massachusetts and the Making of Global Capitalism, 1865–Present" (PhD diss., Harvard University, 2016), 39, fig. 1.2.

6. Massachusetts Constable of the Commonwealth, *Report of the Hon. Henry K. Oliver* (Massachusetts Constable of the Commonwealth, 1868), 23.

7. Massachusetts Constable of the Commonwealth, *Report*, 23.

8. Massachusetts Constable of the Commonwealth, *Report*, 22.

9. Massachusetts Bureau of Statistics of Labor, *Fourteenth Annual Report*, 399.

10. Massachusetts Bureau of Statistics of Labor, *Fourteenth Annual Report*, 401.

Chapter 2

1. David P. Gagan, "The Railroads and the Public, 1870–1881: A Study of Charles Elliott Perkins' Business Ethics," *Business History Review* 39, no. 1 (Spring 1965): 53.

2. Gagan, "The Railroads," 53.

3. Howard Zinn, *A People's History of the United States* (Harper Perennial Modern Classics, 2005), 262.

4. Stuart D. Brandes, *American Welfare Capitalism 1880–1940* (University of Chicago Press, 1976), 2.

5. Brandes, *American Welfare*, 3.

6. Brandes, *American Welfare*, 1–3.

7. "A Brief Overview of the Pullman Story," National Park Service, updated January 10, 2025, https://www.nps.gov/pull/learn/historyculture/a-brief-overview-of-the-pullman-story.htm.

8. "The Parable of Pullman," Illinois Labor History Society, January 22, 2016, https://www.illinoislaborhistory.org/labor-history-articles/the-parable-of-pullman.

9. Zinn, *A People's History*, 280; "United States Strike Commission: Pullman's Palace Car Company," Illinois State Museum, accessed January 10, 2025, https://exhibits.museum.state.il.us/exhibits/athome/1850/voices/curtis/car.htm.

10. "The Parable of Pullman," Illinois Labor History Society.

Chapter 3

1. Lee Soltow, *Distribution of Wealth and Income in the United States in 1798* (University of Pittsburgh Press, 1989), 283, table 89.

2. Jeffrey G. Williamson and Peter H. Lindert, "Long-Term Trends in American Wealth Inequality," in *Modeling the Distribution and Intergenerational Transmission of Wealth*, ed. James D. Smith (University of Chicago Press, 1980), 57, table 1.15.

3. Thomas Piketty homepage, Paris School of Economics, figs. I.1, 10.6, accessed January 11, 2025, http://piketty.pse.ens.fr/files/capital21c/en/Piketty2014FiguresTables.pdf.

4. Williamson and Lindert, "Long-Term Trends," table 1.15.

5. John A. Ryan, *A Living Wage: Its Ethical and Economic Aspects* (Macmillan Company, 1912), 3.

6. Ryan, *A Living Wage*, 123, 138, 150.

7. Albert Rees, *Real Wages in Manufacturing, 1890–1914* (Princeton University Press, 1961), 32, table 9. Data is interpolated; John Iceland, *Poverty in America: A Handbook* (University of California Press, 2013), 14.

8. Morrell Heald, *The Social Responsibilities of Business* (Press of Case Western Reserve University, 1970), 28.

9. Michael McGerr, *A Fierce Discontent: The Rise and Fall of the Progressive Movement in America, 1870–1920* (Free Press, 2003), 68.

10. McGerr, *A Fierce Discontent*, 68.

11. "Handbook of the National Association of Manufacturers," 1907, incorporated into Select Committee of the House of Representatives Appointed Under House

Resolution 198, *Hearings Before the Select Committee of the House of Representatives Appointed Under House Resolution 198, Sixty-Third Congress First Session*, vol. 10, pt. 29–30 (Government Printing Office, 1913), 2585, https://babel.hathitrust.org/cgi/pt?id=coo.31924054280965&seq=138.

12. McGerr, *A Fierce Discontent*, 164.

13. Murray N. Rothbard, *The Progressive Era* (Mises Institute, 2017), 242; Donna J. Wood, "The Strategic Use of Public Policy: Business Support for the 1906 Food and Drug Act," *Business History Review* 59, no. 3 (Autumn 1985): 403, 413.

14. "Mr. Parry Merciless," *Indianapolis Journal* 53, no. 105 (1903), 4, https://newspapers.library.in.gov/?a=d&d=IJ19030415.

15. Samuel Gompers, speech to the American Federal of Labor convention, November 1903, https://gompers.umd.edu/quotes.htm.

16. Heald, *The Social Responsibilities*, 32.

17. Jonathan Rees, "Managing the Mills: Labor Policy in the American Steel Industry, 1892–1937" (PhD diss., University of Wisconsin-Madison, 1997) is the source for information on US Steel's welfare capitalism program. Employee housing: 126–127, 152; job safety and twelve-hour day: 140, 178–185; high turnover: 158; stock ownership: 152, 162–171; pensions: 152, 172–177; spies: 109, 114, 192; summary dismissal and blacklist: 101–102, 113, 139; variable production: 122–124, 191; unsupported strikes: 101, 107.

18. Stuart D. Brandes, *American Welfare Capitalism 1880–1940* (University of Chicago Press, 1976), 138–139.

19. Brandes, *American Welfare*, 28.

20. Piketty homepage, fig. I.1.

21. US Bureau of the Census, *Historical Statistics of the United States, Colonial Times to 1957* (US Bureau of the Census, 1960), chap. D, 92, https://www.census.gov/library/publications/1960/compendia/hist_stats_colonial-1957.html.

22. Paul D. Romero and Julie Whittaker, *A Brief Examination of Union Membership Data* (Congressional Research Service, 2023), 4, fig.1, https://sgp.fas.org/crs/misc/R47596.pdf.

Chapter 4

1. Barry Eichengreen and Kris Mitchener, "The Great Depression as a Credit Boom Gone Wrong," Working Paper No. 137 (Bank for International Settlements, September 2003), https://www.bis.org/publ/work137.pdf.

2. Michael Hiltzik, "They Tried to Call FDR and the New Deal 'Socialist' Too. Here's How He Responded," *Los Angeles Times*, February 13, 2019, https://www.latimes.com/business/hiltzik/la-fi-hiltzik-socialism-20190213-story.html.

3. "Percent Change from Preceding Period in Real Gross Domestic Product," Bureau of Economic Analysis, table 1.1.1, accessed October 4, 2024, https://www.bea.gov/itable/.

4. Chad Stone et al., "A Guide to Statistics on Historical Trends in Income Inequality," Center on Budget and Policy Priorities, updated January 13, 2020, https://www.cbpp.org/sites/default/files/atoms/files/11-28-11pov_0.pdf.

5. Thomas Piketty homepage, Paris School of Economics, figs. I.1, 10.6, accessed January 11, 2025, http://piketty.pse.ens.fr/files/capital21c/en/Piketty2014FiguresTables.pdf.

6. A major exception was healthcare. The powerful American Medical Association, which feared reduction in doctors' fees, resolutely opposed government health insurance. But during World War II, when competition for labor was fierce and wages controlled, company-provided healthcare could count as a proxy for compensation in attracting and retaining needed workers since it counted neither toward the wage cap nor as taxable income to the employee. We are still dealing with the consequences of this expedient policy.

7. Nick Bunker, "A Post-War History of US Economic Growth," Washington Center for Equitable Growth, July 2014, 5, fig. 2, https://equitablegrowth.org/post-war-history-u-s-economic-growth/.

8. Laura Feiveson, "Labor Unions and the US Economy," US Department of the Treasury, August 28, 2023, https://home.treasury.gov/news/featured-stories/labor-unions-and-the-us-economy.

9. Leland L. Doan, "Fundamental Role of Business Is to Operate Profitably," *Commercial and Financial Chronicle*, July 18, 1957, 18.

10. Andrew Hacker, "Do Corporations Have a Social Duty?," *New York Times Magazine*, November 17, 1963, 11.

11. Hacker, "Do Corporations Have a Social Duty?"

12. Gina-Gail S. Fletcher and H. Timothy Lovelace Jr., "Corporate Racial Responsibility," *Columbia Law Review* 124, no. 2 (2024): 361, 365–367.

13. David Hasemyer et al., "For Oil Industry, Clean Air Fight Was Dress Rehearsal for Climate Denial," Inside Climate News, June 6, 2016, https://insideclimatenews.org/news/06062016/oil-industry-clean-air-fight-smog-los-angeles-dress-rehearsal-climate-change-denial-exxon/.

14. "Benefits and Costs of the Clean Air Amendments of 1990," Environmental Protection Agency, July 2015, https://www.epa.gov/sites/default/files/2015-07/documents/factsheet.pdf.

Chapter 5

1. Milton Friedman, "The Social Responsibility of Business Is to Increase Its Profits," *New York Times Magazine*, September 13, 1970.

2. Robert S. McIntyre and Robert Folan, "Corporate Income Taxes in the Reagan Years," Citizens for Tax Justice, October 1984, https://ctj.sfo2.digitaloceanspaces.com/pdf/1984ReaganYears.pdf.

3. Lawrence A. Sullivan and Wolfgang Fikentscher, "On the Growth of the Antitrust Idea," *Berkeley Journal of International Law* 16, no. 2 (December 1998): 206–207.

4. "Modern Antitrust Enforcement," Yale School of Management, Thurman Arnold Project, figs. 1, 2, last updated June 22, 2020, https://som.yale.edu/centers/thurman-arnold-project-at-yale/modern-antitrust-enforcement.

5. Donna Sockell and John Thomas Delany, "Union Organizing and the Reagan NLRB," *Contemporary Policy Issues* 5 (October 1987): 28, 40–43.

6. Spencer Rich, "'Safety Net' Strands Thinner Under Reagan," *Washington Post*, November 27, 1988, https://www.washingtonpost.com/archive/politics/1988/11/27/safety-net-strands-thinner-under-reagan/74e881aa-072a-4e41-96a2-0e2f3744689c/.

7. Thomas Piketty homepage, Paris School of Economics, fig. I.1, accessed January 11, 2025, http://piketty.pse.ens.fr/files/capital21c/en/Piketty2014FiguresTables.pdf.

8. "Union Membership and Income Inequality," Center for Economic and Policy Research, September 9, 2015, https://cepr.net/publications/union-membership-and-income-inequality/; "Union Members—2023," Bureau of Labor Statistics, January 23, 2024, https://www.bls.gov/news.release/pdf/union2.pdf.

9. Lawrence Mishel et al., "Wage Stagnation in Nine Charts," Economic Policy Institute, January 6, 2015, fig. 2, https://www.epi.org/publication/charting-wage-stagnation/.

10. Mishel et al., "Wage Stagnation," fig. 4.

11. David Cooper et al., "The Value of the Federal Minimum Wage Is at Its Lowest Point in 55 Years," *Working Economics Blog* (Economic Policy Institute), https://www.epi.org/blog/the-value-of-the-federal-minimum-wage-is-at-its-lowest-point-in-66-years/.

12. "Corporate Profit Margin (After Tax)," GuruFocus, last updated October 1, 2024, https://www.gurufocus.com/economic_indicators/62/corporate-profit-margin-after-tax-.

13. "The United States Has a Market Concentration Problem," Roosevelt Institute, July 2020, 1, https://rooseveltinstitute.org/wp-content/uploads/2020/07/RI-US-market-concentration-problem-brief-201809.pdf.

14. "Modern Antitrust Enforcement," Yale School of Management.

15. Heather Boushey and Helen Knudsen, "The Importance of Competition for the American Economy," The White House, July 9, 2021, https://www.whitehouse.gov/cea/written-materials/2021/07/09/the-importance-of-competition-for-the-american-economy/#_ftn3.

16. Lawrence Mishel and Jori Kandra, "CEO Pay Has Skyrocketed 1,322% Since 1978," Economic Policy Institute, August 10, 2021, https://www.epi.org/publication/ceo-pay-in-2020/.

17. Marcus Lu, "Visualizing Wealth Distribution in America (1990–2023)," Visual Capitalist, February 19, 2024, https://www.visualcapitalist.com/wealth-distribution-in-america/.

18. Piketty homepage, fig. I.1.

19. Lu, "Visualizing Wealth Distribution."

20. Peter H. Lindert and Jeffrey G. Williamson, *Unequal Gains: American Growth and Inequality Since 1700* (Princeton University Press, 2016), 119.

21. "Business Roundtable Redefines the Purpose of a Corporation to Promote 'An Economy That Serves All Americans," Business Roundtable, August 19, 2019, https://www.businessroundtable.org/business-roundtable-redefines-the-purpose-of-a-corporation-to-promote-an-economy-that-serves-all-americans.

22. Morrell Heald, *The Social Responsibilities of Business* (Press of Case Western Reserve University, 1970), 32.

23. Aneesh Raghunandan and Shiva Rajgopal, "Do Socially Responsible Firms Walk the Talk?," *Journal of Law and Economics* 67, no. 4 (2024), https://doi.org/10.1086/728855.

Chapter 6

1. K. Michael Cummings et al., "Failed Promises of the Cigarette Industry and Its Effect on Consumer Misperceptions About the Health Risks of Smoking," *Tobacco Control* 11 (2002): i110–i117, https://pubmed.ncbi.nlm.nih.gov/11893821/.

2. Cummings et al., "Failed Promises."

3. "The 1964 Report on Smoking and Health," National Library of Medicine, accessed October 4, 2024, https://profiles.nlm.nih.gov/spotlight/nn/feature/smoking.

4. "Per Capita Cigarette Consumption in the United States from 1900–2015," Statista.com, accessed October 4, 2024, https://www.statista.com/statistics/261576/cigarette-consumption-per-adult-in-the-us/.

5. "Tobacco Industry Research Committee," Tobacco Tactics at the University of Bath, February 7, 2020, https://www.tobaccotactics.org/article/tobacco-industry-research-committee/.

6. Cummings et al., "Failed Promises."

7. Cummings et al., "Failed Promises."

8. Cummings et al., "Failed Promises."

9. Cristin E. Kearns et al., "Sugar Industry and Coronary Heart Disease Research: A Historical Analysis of Internal Industry Documents," *JAMA Internal Medicine* 176, no. 1 (2016): 1680–1685, https://pubmed.ncbi.nlm.nih.gov/27617709/.

10. Alison Moodie, "Before You Read Another Health Study, Check Who's Funding the Research," *Guardian*, December 12, 2016, https://www.theguardian.com/lifeandstyle/2016/dec/12/studies-health-nutrition-sugar-coca-cola-marion-nestle.

11. Tony Briscoe, "Exxon Mobil Publicly Denied Global Warming but Quietly Predicted It," *Los Angeles Times*, January 12, 2023, https://www.latimes.com/environment/story/2023-01-12/exxonmobil-accurately-predicted-effects-of-global-warming.

12. Roger Rosenblatt, "How Do Tobacco Executives Live with Themselves?," *New York Times Magazine*, March 20, 1994, https://www.nytimes.com/1994/03/20/magazine/how-do-tobacco-executives-live-with-themselves.html. All quotes from Philip Morris executives in this section come from this article.

13. William H. Whyte Jr., "Groupthink," *Fortune*, March 1, 1952, https://fortune.com/article/groupthink-fortune-1952/.

14. Irving L. Janis, "Groupthink," *Psychology Today*, November 1971, https://agcommtheory.pbworks.com/f/GroupThink.pdf.

15. James D. Rose, "Diverse Perspectives on the Groupthink Theory—A Literary Review," *Emerging Leadership Journeys* 4, no. 1 (2011), https://www.regent.edu/journal/emerging-leadership-journeys/groupthink-theory/.

Chapter 7

1. Pieter Jan Trinks and Bert Scholtens, "The Opportunity Cost of Negative Screening in Socially Responsible Investing," *Journal of Business Ethics* 140 (May 2015): 193–208, https://link.springer.com/article/10.1007/s10551-015-2684-3.

2. Jeremy Salvucci, "Institutional Investors: Who They Are & What They Do," TheStreet, April 8, 2024, https://www.thestreet.com/dictionary/institutional-investors.

3. UN Global Compact, *Who Cares Wins: Connecting Financial Markets to a Changing World* (UN Global Compact, 2004), https://d306pr3pise04h.cloudfront.net/docs/issues_doc%2FFinancial_markets%2Fwho_cares_who_wins.pdf.

4. "Introducing the Goldman Sachs Energy Environmental and Social Index," Goldman Sachs, February 24, 2004, 2, 6, accessed June 6, 2024, https://www.unepfi.org/fileadmin/documents/materiality1/eesi_goldman_sachs_2004.pdf.

5. UN Global Compact, *Who Cares Wins*, 12–18.

6. US SIF Foundation, *2022 Report on US Sustainable Investing Trends* (US SIF Foundation, 2022), https://www.ussif.org//Files/Trends/2022/Trends%202022%20Executive%20Summary.pdf.

7. Global Sustainable Investment Alliance, *Global Sustainable Investment Review 2022* (Global Sustainable Investment Alliance, 2023), https://www.gsi-alliance.org/wp-content/uploads/2023/12/GSIA-Report-2022.pdf.

8. US SIF Foundation, *2022 Report*, fig. 2.13.

9. Lydia Saad, "ESG Not Making Waves with American Public," Gallup, May 22, 2023, https://news.gallup.com/poll/506171/esg-not-making-waves-american-public.aspx.

10. "Building More Resilient Portfolios," BlackRock, accessed July 10, 2024, https://www.blackrock.com/lu/intermediaries/themes/sustainable-investing/esg-integration#.

11. Aymen Karoui et al., *ESG Risk Ratings: A 360° Review* (Morningstar Sustainalytics, 2023), https://connect.sustainalytics.com/hubfs/INV/Ebooks/ESG%20Risk%20Ratings%20-%20360%20Report%20eBook/MS_ESG_RR_360_Review_Ebook_Final.pdf.

12. MSCI, *MSCI ESG Ratings Methodology: Executive Summary* (November 2020), https://fintech.mcu.edu.tw/wp-content/uploads/sites/42/2023/02/MSCI-ESG-Ratings-Methodology-Exec-Summary-Nov-2020.pdf; emphasis added.

13. I tried to clarify with MSCI the implications of their principles, asking, for example, whether a company's ESG rating would be affected if there were no financial liability for its continued use of a harmful chemical. They kindly sent a lengthy response, largely rephrasing their methodology document. They confirmed that "MSCI ESG Ratings provide an opinion of companies' management of financially relevant ESG risks and opportunities" but declined to answer yes or no to my hypothetical case, saying that the answer was "more nuanced."

14. The rating information in this chapter is taken from the rating agencies' websites, where they publicly disclose ratings for all the companies they rate, accessed August 2024. See MSCI: https://www.msci.com/our-solutions/esg-investing/esg-ratings-climate-search-tool; Sustainalytics: https://www.sustainalytics.com/esg-ratings; and ISS-ESG: https://www.iss-corporate.com/solutions/esg-solutions/iss-esg-gateway/.

15. For MSCI's interpretation of "water stress," see Cam Simpson et al., "The ESG Mirage," Bloomberg, December 10, 2021, https://www.bloomberg.com/graphics/2021-what-is-esg-investing-msci-ratings-focus-on-corporate-bottom-line/.

16. "Prospectus, Supplement Dated Sep. 1, 2023," Victory Sustainable World Fund, 17, accessed May 28, 2024, https://vcm.onlineprospectus.net/VCM/USAAWG/index.php?ctype=prospectus; "Holdings as of June 30, 2024," Victory Sustainable World Fund, updated December 31, 2024, https://vcm.com/assets/victoryMF/allholdings-pdf/Victory_World_Growth_Fund_Holdings.pdf.

17. Polly Bindman, "Why ESG Funds Are Full of Fossil Fuels," Energy Monitor, April 28, 2023, https://www.energymonitor.ai/finance/sustainable-finance/why-esg-funds-are-full-of-fossil-fuels-but-thats-okay/.

Chapter 8

1. Benchmark Digital Partners, *The 2022 Benchmark ESG Survey: Investor Attitudes on Company ESG Data* (Benchmark Digital Partners, 2023), https://benchmarkgensuite.com/lp-the-2022-benchmark-esg-survey-exploring-business-leaders-impressions-of-their-esg-programs/.

2. Alex Edmans et al., "Sustainable Investing: Evidence from the Field," Working Paper No. 1028/2024 (European Corporate Governance Institute, September 20, 2024), https://papers.ssrn.com/sol3/papers.cfm?abstract_id=4963062.

3. Moore Intelligence, *The $4 Trillion ESG Dividend* (Moore Intelligence, 2022), https://www.moore-global.com/MediaLibsAndFiles/media/MooreStephens2020/Documents/Moore_ESG_White-Paper_FINAL.pdf.

4. For a good guide to the multiform biases in academic research for the nonexpert, see Alex Edmans, *May Contain Lies: How Stories, Statistics, and Studies Exploit Our Biases—And What We Can Do About It* (University of California Press, 2024).

5. "Sustainability Services," Moore Global, accessed October 3, 2024, https://www.moore-global.com/industries/sustainability-services.

6. Gordon L. Clark et al., *From the Stockholder to the Stakeholder* (Oxford University and Arabesque Asset Management, 2015), https://papers.ssrn.com/sol3/papers.cfm?abstract_id=2508281. The report also covers ESG effects on stock prices, but for this chapter, I used only the papers related to company financial performance.

7. Clark et al., *From the Stockholder to the Stakeholder*, 8.

8. Rob Bauer and Daniel Hann, "Corporate Environmental Management and Credit Risk," Working Paper (Maastricht University and European Centre for Corporate Engagement, June 30, 2010), https://papers.ssrn.com/sol3/papers.cfm?abstract_id=1660470.

9. Lee E. Preston and Douglas P. O'Bannon, "The Corporate Social-Financial Performance Relationship," *Business and Society* 36, no. 4 (December 1997): 419–429.

10. Marc B. J. Schauten and Dick van Dijk, "Corporate Governance and the Cost of Debt of Large European Firms," Research in Management, October 2011, http://hdl.handle.net/1765/19679.

11. "Lifting Financial Performance by Investing in Women," BlackRock, November 2023, https://www.blackrock.com/corporate/literature/whitepaper/lifting-financial-performance-by-investing-in-women.pdf.

12. Alex Edmans, "Does Gender Diversity Really Boost Financial Performance?," November 2, 2023, https://maycontainlies.com/does-gender-diversity-really-boost-financial-performance/.

13. Alex Edmans, Caroline Flammer, and Simon Glossner, "(Diversity) Equity and Inclusion," April 17, 2025, https://papers.ssrn.com/sol3/papers.cfm?abstract_id=4426488.

14. Edmans, "Gender Diversity."

Chapter 9

1. Jan-Carol Plagge and Douglas Grim, "Have Investors Paid a Performance Price? Examining the Behavior of ESG Equity Funds," *Journal of Portfolio Management* 46, no. 3 (February 2020): 1–18.

2. Information sources for case study, all accessed 2–3Q 2024:

Fund and index factsheets:

ESGU: https://www.ishares.com/us/literature/fact-sheet/esgu-ishares-esg-aware-msci-usa-etf-fund-fact-sheet-en-us.pdf

PBUS: https://www.invesco.com/us-rest/contentdetail?contentId=36f1f78b6e47f510VgnVCM100000c2f1bf0aRCRD&dnsName=us

MSCI ESG Index: https://www.msci.com/documents/10199/255599/msci-usa-extended-esg-focus-index-usd-gross.pdf

MSCI USA Index: https://www.msci.com/documents/10199/255599/msci-usa-index-gross.pdf

MSCI Index methodology: https://www.msci.com/index/methodology/latest/ExtendedESGFocus

MSCI online ratings tool: https://www.msci.com/our-solutions/esg-investing/esg-fund-ratings-climate-search-tool/funds

Morningstar online ratings tool: https://www.morningstar.com/

Fund overlap tool: ETF Research Center, https://www.etfrc.com/funds/overlap.php

3. Zachary Evans and Bryan Armour, "2023 US Fund Fee Study," Morningstar Manager Research, July 2024, https://assets.contentstack.io/v3/assets/blt4eb669caa7dc65b2/blt7b54038c40308f13/668c241bcf6f65d1556e706b/2023_US_Fund_Fee_Study.pdf.

4. Note that "tracking error" is not mathematically identical to the gross return divergence between a fund and its benchmark over a selected time period, but the two are close enough to be used interchangeably in nontechnical works like this.

5. Evans and Armour, "2023 US Fund Fee Study."

6. Barbara Friedberg and Paul Katzoff, "The Best ESG Funds of August 2024," *Forbes*, July 1, 2024, https://www.forbes.com/advisor/investing/best-esg-funds/.

7. Comparison data is available upon request: jswanso4@gmu.edu.

8. Giovanni Bruno et al., "'Honey, I Shrunk the ESG Alpha': Risk-Adjusting ESG Portfolio Returns," Scientific Beta, April 2021, https://cdn.ihsmarkit.com/www/pdf/0521/Honey-I-Shrunk-the-ESG-Alpha.pdf.

Chapter 10

1. Gill Lofts, "How ESG Data Markets Have Evolved for Financial Services," EY, March 21, 2023, https://www.ey.com/en_gl/financial-services-emeia/how-esg-data-markets-have-evolved-for-financial-services#.

2. "Rate the Raters 2023: ESG Ratings at a Crossroads," The Sustainability Institute, March 2023, https://www.sustainability.com/globalassets/sustainability.com/thinking/pdfs/2023/rate-the-raters-report-april-2023.pdf.

3. For McDonald's case study and ESG ratings upgrade data, see Cam Simpson et al., "The ESG Mirage," Bloomberg, December 10, 2021, https://www.bloomberg.com/graphics/2021-what-is-esg-investing-msci-ratings-focus-on-corporate-bottom-line/.

4. Ross Kerber and Michael Flaherty, "Investing with 'Green' Ratings? It's a Gray Area," Reuters, June 26, 2017, https://www.reuters.com/article/us-climate-ratings-analysis-idUSKBN19H0DM/.

5. Michael J. LaBella, "The Devil Is in the Details: The Divergence in ESG Data and Its Implications for Responsible Investing," QS Investors, September 2019, https://qsinvestorsproduction.blob.core.windows.net/media/Default/PDF/The%20Devil%20is%20in%20the%20Details_Divergence%20in%20ESG%20Data.pdf.

6. LaBella, "The Devil Is in the Details."

7. LaBella, "The Devil Is in the Details," exh. 1.

8. Florian Berg et al., "Aggregate Confusion: The Divergence of ESG Ratings," *Review of Finance* 26, no. 6 (2022): 1315–1344, https://doi.org/10.1093/rof/rfac033.

Chapter 11

1. "Reenergize ExxonMobil Investor Presentation," Engine No. 1, May 2021, https://reenergizexom.com/documents/Investor-Presentation-May-2021-v2.pdf.

2. Robert G. Eccles and Colin Mayer, "Can a Tiny Hedge Fund Push ExxonMobil Towards Sustainability?," *Harvard Business Review*, January 20, 2021, https://hbr.org/2021/01/can-a-tiny-hedge-fund-push-exxonmobile-towards-sustainability?ab=hero-subleft-1.

3. Matt Phillips, "Exxon's Board Defeat Signals the Rise of Social-Good Activists," *New York Times*, June 9, 2021, https://www.nytimes.com/2021/06/09/business/exxon-mobil-engine-no1-activist.html.

4. "ExxonMobil: Strengthening Global Energy Security," *Focus Outlook*, August 2022, p. 26, https://focusoutlook.com/magazine/Top-10-Oil-and-Gas-Innovators-2022/#page=27.

5. Clifford Krauss, "Exxon Mobil Strikes $60 Billion Deal for Shale Giant," *New York Times*, October 11, 2023, https://www.nytimes.com/2023/10/11/business/economy/exxon-mobil-pioneer-natural-resources.html.

6. Swagath Bandhakavi, "ExxonMobil's Q3 2024 Net Income Drops by 5% to $8.6bn," NS Energy, November 4, 2024, https://www.nsenergybusiness.com/news/exxonmobils-q3-2024-net-income-drops-by-5-to-8-6bn/.

7. "ExxonMobil Announces Plans to 2030 That Build on Its Unique Advantages," ExxonMobil Corp., December 11, 2024, https://corporate.exxonmobil.com/news/news-releases/2024/1211_exxonmobil-announces-plans-to-2030-that-build-on-its-unique-advantages.

8. "Brent Crude Oil Prices—10 Year Daily Chart," Macrotrends, accessed September 24, 2024, https://www.macrotrends.net/2480/brent-crude-oil-prices-10-year-daily-chart.

9. "Fossil Fuel CO2 Emissions Increase Again in 2024," University of Reading, November 13, 2024, https://www.reading.ac.uk/news/2024/Research-News/Fossil-fuel-CO2-emissions-increase-again-in-2024#:~:text=With%20projected%20emissions%20from%20land,40.6%20billion%20tonnes%20last%20year.

10. "Energy Supply," ExxonMobil Corp., August 26, 2024, https://corporate.exxonmobil.com/sustainability-and-reports/global-outlook/energy-supply.

11. "Net Zero Roadmap: A Global Pathway to Keep the 1.5 °C Goal in Reach," International Energy Agency, revised November 2024, fig. 2.12, https://iea.blob.core.windows.net/assets/8ad619b9-17aa-473d-8a2f-4b90846f5c19/NetZeroRoadmap_AGlobalPathwaytoKeepthe1.5CGoalinReach-2023Update.pdf.

12. "ExxonMobil Announces Plans," ExxonMobil Corp. The comparison is "cash capex" to "lower emissions investment opportunities," in both cases averaged over 2025–2030.

13. Dan Weil, "Analysts Revamp ExxonMobil Stock Price Targets After Oil Surges," TheStreet, April 6, 2024, https://www.thestreet.com/investing/stocks/analysts-revamp-exxonmobil-stock-price-targets-after-oil-surges.

14. "ExxonMobil: One Year Later," Engine No.1, May 25, 2022, https://engine1.com/transforming/articles/exxon-mobil-one-year-later/; emphasis added.

15. Richard Marens, "Inventing Corporate Governance: The Mid-Century Emergence of Shareholder Activism," *Journal of Business and Management* 8, no. 4 (Fall 2002): 365–389.

16. Elaine X. Grant, "TWA—The Death of a Legend," *St. Louis Magazine*, July 28, 2006, https://www.stlmag.com/TWA-A-Seath-Of-A-Legend/.

17. "Annual Review of Shareholder Activism 2023," Lazard, January 8, 2024, https://www.lazard.com/research-insights/annual-review-of-shareholder-activism-2023/.

18. Mark R. DesJardine and Rodolphe Durand, "Disentangling the Effects of Hedge Fund Activism on Firm Financial and Social Performance," *Strategic Management Journal* 41, no. 6 (2020): 1054–1082, https://doi.org/10.1002/smj.3126.

19. DesJardine and Durand, "Disentangling the Effects."

20. "2024 Proxy Season Review: Part 1," Sullivan & Cromwell LLP, August 13, 2024, https://www.sullcrom.com/insights/memo/2024/August/2024-Proxy-Season-Review-Part-1.

21. Interfaith Center on Corporate Responsibility, *ICCR's 2024 Proxy Resolution & Voting Guide* (Interfaith Center on Corporate Responsibility, 2024), https://www.iccr.org/reports/iccrs-2024-proxy-resolutions-voting-guide/.

22. "2024 Proxy Season," Sullivan, 1.

23. See, for example, Jeremy Salvucci, "Institutional Investors: Who They Are & What They Do," TheStreet, April 8, 2024, https://www.thestreet.com/dictionary/institutional-investors.

24. BlackRock, *Investment Stewardship Annual Report: January 1–December 31, 2023* (BlackRock, 2024), https://www.blackrock.com/corporate/literature/publication/annual-stewardship-report-2023-summary.pdf.

25. "Annual Review of Shareholder Activism 2023," Lazard.

26. Abhijay Sood et al., *Voting Matters 2023* (ShareAction, 2024), https://cdn2.assets-servd.host/shareaction-api/production/resources/reports/Voting-Matters-2023.pdf.

27. Sarah E. Hunt, "Why the ESG Battleground Must Shift from Asset Managers to Proxy Advisors," Real Clear Policy, September 21, 2023, https://www.realclearpolicy.com/articles/2023/09/21/why_the_esg_battleground_must_shift_from_asset_managers_to_proxy_advisors_981133.html.

28. "Global Fossil Fuel Divestment Commitments Database," Stand.earth, accessed January 25, 2025, https://divestmentdatabase.org/.

29. Siew Hong Teoh et al., "The Effect of Socially Activist Investment Policies on the Financial Markets: Evidence from the South African Boycott," *Journal of Business* 72, no. 1 (1999): 35–89, https://doi.org/10.1086/209602.

30. Catherine Barnes, "International Isolation and Pressure for Change in South Africa," *Accord*, no. 19 (February 2008), https://www.c-r.org/accord/incentives-sanctions-and-conditionality/international-isolation-and-pressure-change-south.

31. Atif Ansar et al., *Stranded Assets and the Fossil Fuel Divestment Campaign: What Does Divestment Mean for the Valuation of Fossil Fuel Assets?* (Smith School of Enterprise and the Environment, University of Oxford, 2013), https://www.smithschool.ox.ac.uk/sites/default/files/2022-03/SAP-divestment-report-final.pdf.

32. Jonathan B. Berk and Jules H. van Binsbergen, "The Impact of Impact Investing," *Journal of Financial Economics* 164 (2025), https://doi.org/10.1016/j.jfineco.2024.103972.

Chapter 12

1. Kanishka Singh, "SEC Charges Goldman Sachs Asset Management with Not Following ESG Investments Policies," Reuters, November 22, 2022, https://www.reuters.com/world/us/sec-charges-goldman-sachs-asset-management-not-following-esg-investments-2022-11-22/#.

2. Patricia Kowsmann and Ken Brown, "Fired Executive Says Deutsche Bank's DWS Overstated Sustainable-Investing Efforts," *Wall Street Journal*, August 1, 2021, https://www.wsj.com/articles/fired-executive-says-deutsche-banks-dws-overstated-sustainable-investing-efforts-11627810380.

3. "Deutsche Bank Subsidiary DWS to Pay $25 Million for Anti-Money Laundering Violations and Misstatements Regarding ESG Investments," press release, Securities and Exchange Commission, September 25, 2023, https://www.sec.gov/news/press-release/2023-194.

4. "SEC Charges Brazilian Mining Company with Misleading Investors About Safety Prior to Deadly Dam Collapse," press release, Securities and Exchange Commission, April 28, 2022, https://www.sec.gov/newsroom/press-releases/2022-72.

5. "We Are Not the Securities and Environment Commission—At Least Not Yet," statement by Commissioner Hester M. Peirce, U.S. Securities and Exchange

Commission, March 21, 2022, https://www.sec.gov/newsroom/speeches-statements/peirce-climate-disclosure-20220321.

6. *State of Iowa et al. v. Securities and Exchange Commission*, No. 24–1522 (8th Cir.), State Petitioners' Emergency Motion, April 3, 2024.

7. "Comments of the Competitive Enterprise Institute, Caesar Rodney Institute, Committee for a Constructive Tomorrow (CFACT), Energy and Environment Legal Institute, FreedomWorks, Heartland Institute, National Center for Public Policy Research, and 60 Plus Association," Competitive Enterprise Institute, June 11, 2011, https://cei.org/wp-content/uploads/2021/06/Climate-Risk-Disclosure-Marlo-Lewis-CEI-Free-Market-Groups-6-11-2021-updated-6-14-2021.pdf.

8. Renate de Lange et al., "The Promise and Reality of CSRD Reporting," PwC, June 13, 2024, https://www.pwc.com/gx/en/issues/esg/global-csrd-survey.html.

9. "Sustainable Finance," newsletter, Directorate-General for Financial Stability, Financial Services and Capital Markets Union, May 21, 2025, https://finance.ec.europa.eu/news/sustainable-finance-2025-05-21_en.

10. European Commission, *Summary Report of the Open and Targeted Consultations on the SFDR Assessment, 14 September 2023–22 December 2023* (European Commission, 2024), https://finance.ec.europa.eu/document/download/0f2cfde1-12b0-4860-b548-0393ac5b592b_en?filename=2023-sfdr-implementation-summary-of-responses_en.pdf.

11. "Sustainable Finance."

12. "SFDR Article 8 and Article 9 Funds: Q4 2024 in Review," Morningstar Sustainalytics, July 25, 2024, https://assets.contentstack.io/v3/assets/blt4eb669caa7dc65b2/blte62ae82a4889fb9e/67997cb0e4273c33b8b87f51/SFDR_Article_8_and_Article_9_Funds_Q4_2024_.pdf.

13. Robert E. Furdak, "ESG Performance and Flows: From a Tale of Two Cities in 2023 to (Hopefully!) Great Expectations in 2024," Man Institute, January 25, 2024, https://www.man.com/maninstitute/ESG-performance-and-flows.

14. EFAMA, "ESG Ratings of Article 8 and 9 Funds," *Market Insights*, no. 11 (October 2022), https://www.efama.org/newsroom/news/market-esg-ratings-should-be-transparent-and-competitive-market-insights-issue-11.

Chapter 13

1. Consumers' Research, *Defeating the ESG Attack on the American Free Enterprise System* (Consumers' Research, 2023), https://consumersresearch.org/wp-content/uploads/2023/05/CR_Defeating-the-ESG-White-Paper_Final.pdf.

2. Mike Pence, "Republicans Can Stop ESG Political Bias," *Wall Street Journal*, May 26, 2022, https://www.wsj.com/articles/only-republicans-can-stop-the-esg-madness-woke-musk-consumer-demand-free-speech-corporate-america-11653574189.

3. Pleiades Strategy, *2024 Statehouse Report* (Pleiades Strategy, 2024), https://drive.usercontent.google.com/download?id=1e1PkwVGbMPb7ZhI1W3CYxNce3jJWHBmY&authuser=0&acrobatPromotionSource=GoogleDriveNativeView.

4. Larry Fink's past letters cannot be easily found on the internet as BlackRock has disabled links to most of them. As of October 2024, the 2024 letter is available at https://www.blackrock.com/corporate/investor-relations/larry-fink-annual-chairmans-letter. Some third parties post versions of the letters, but their authenticity is not always assured. All quotes from Larry Fink's letters in this section come from BlackRock itself or other reputable sources that reposted the letters verbatim.

5. Ross Douthat, "The Rise of Woke Capital," *New York Times*, February 28, 2018, https://www.nytimes.com/2018/02/28/opinion/corporate-america-activism.html.

6. Sprout Social, *Championing Change in the Age of Social Media* (Sprout Social, 2018), https://media.sproutsocial.com/pdf/Sprout-Data-Report-Championing-Change-in-the-Age-of-Social-Media.pdf.

7. Shaun Harper, "Where Is the $200 Billion Companies Promised After George Floyd's Murder?," *Forbes*, October 17, 2022, https://www.forbes.com/sites/shaunharper/2022/10/17/where-is-the-200-billion-companies-promised-after-george-floyds-murder/.

8. Alan Rappeport et al., "Corporations Donated Millions to Lawmakers Who Voted to Overturn Election Results," *New York Times*, January 6, 2022, https://www.nytimes.com/2022/01/06/us/politics/congress-corporate-donations-2020-election-overturn.html.

9. Leslie Josephs, "Delta CEO Blasts Georgia Voting Law as 'Unacceptable' and 'Based on a Lie' After Backlash," CNBC, March 31, 2021, https://www.cnbc.com/2021/03/31/delta-ceo-blasts-georgia-voting-law-after-backlash-on-social-media.html.

10. "McConnell Warns 'Stupid' Business Leaders off Political Speech: 'Republicans Drink Coca-Cola, Too," CBS News, April 7, 2021, https://www.cbsnews.com/news/mcconnell-georgia-voting-law-business-leaders-political-speech/.

11. "From Handshake to Clenched Fist," *The Economist*, April 17, 2021, https://www.economist.com/business/2021/04/14/ceo-activism-in-america-is-risky-business.

12. Nicholas Liu, "Disney Is Once Again Giving Money to Anti-LGBTQ+ Republicans Who Passed the 'Don't Say Gay' Law," Salon, June 13, 2024, https://www.salon.com/2024/06/13/disney-is-once-again-giving-money-to-anti-lgbtq-passed-the-dont-say-gay-law/.

13. Tracy Jan et al., "Corporate America's $50 Billion Promise," *Washington Post*, August 23, 2021, https://www.washingtonpost.com/business/interactive/2021/george-floyd-corporate-america-racial-justice/.

14. Anna Bahney, "Homeownership Gap Between Black and White Owners Is Worse Now than a Decade Ago," CNN, February 20, 2024, https://www.cnn.com/2024/02/20/economy/black-white-homeownership-gap/index.html.

15. Olivia Knight, *Racial Justice Scorecard: Large-Cap 3000* (As You Sow, 2024), https://www.asyousow.org/report-page/racial-justice.

16. Edelman Trust Institute, *Edelman Trust Barometer 2024 Special Report: Business and Racial Justice* (Edelman Trust Institute, 2024), https://www.edelman.com/sites/g/files/aatuss191/files/2024-07/2024%20Edelman%20Trust%20Barometer%20Special%20Report%20Business%20and%20Racial%20Justice.pdf.

17. "2024 Proxy Season Review: Part 1," Sullivan & Cromwell LLP, August 13, 2024, https://www.sullcrom.com/insights/memo/2024/August/2024-Proxy-Season-Review-Part-1.

18. Rappeport et al., "Corporations."

19. Rappeport et al., "Corporations."

20. Rappeport et al., "Corporations."

21. Scott Maxwell, "Did Disney or DeSantis Win Their Big Fight? Yes," *Tampa Bay Times*, April 4, 2024, https://www.tampabay.com/opinion/2024/04/04/did-disney-or-desantis-win-their-big-fight-yes/.

22. Brooks Barnes, "Disney and DeSantis Reach Agreement, Ending Protracted Fight," *New York Times*, June 12, 2024, https://www.nytimes.com/2024/06/12/business/disney-desantis-agreement.html.

23. Liu, "Disney."

Chapter 14

1. Global Impact Investing Network, *2022 Sizing the Impact Investing Market* (Global Impact Investing Network, 2022), https://thegiin.org/publication/research/impact-investing-market-size-2022/.

2. John Zipperer, "Natural Fibers Versus Synthetic Fibers: Patagonia and Levi Strauss Say Organic Cotton 'Sucks,'" August 14, 2013, HuffPost, https://www.huffpost.com/entry/natural-fibers-versus-synthetic_n_3758415.

3. Some impact asset managers have been able to meet regulatory hurdles and can deal directly with retail investors. A notable example is Calvert Impact Capital,

which offers its Community Investment Notes in a variety of maturities: https://calvertimpact.org/investing/community-investment-note.

4. Tameo, *Private Asset Impact Fund Report 2023* (Tameo, 2023), https://www.convergence.finance/resource/private-asset-impact-fund-report-2023/view.

5. Kusi Hornberger, "The Agricultural SME Finance Challenge," Feed the Future, July 25, 2018, https://web.archive.org/web/20250203140512/https://agrilinks.org/post/agricultural-sme-finance-challenge.

6. Jim Bildner, "Impact Investing Can't Deliver by Chasing Market Returns," *Stanford Social Innovation Review*, May 17, 2023, https://ssir.org/articles/entry/impact_investing_cant_deliver_by_chasing_market_returns#.

7. Dean Hand et al., *2023 GIINsight: Impact Investing Allocations, Activity & Performance* (Global Impact Investing Network, 2023), https://thegiin.org/publication/research/2023-giinsight-series/.

8. Dean Hand et al., *2023 GIINsight.*

9. Dean Hand et al., *2023 GIINsight.*

10. International Finance Corporation et al., *DFI Working Group on Blended Concessional Finance for Private Sector Projects* (International Finance Corporation, 2023), https://www.ifc.org/content/dam/ifc/doc/mgrt/2023-03-dfi-bcf-joint-report.pdf.

11. Dean Hand et al., *2023 GIINsight.*

12. Paul Sullivan, "An Argument for Investing Where the Return Is Social Change," *New York Times*, April 5, 2021, https://www.nytimes.com/2021/04/02/your-money/impact-investing-social-change.html.

13. Sara Balitzky and Natacha Mosson, "Impact Investing—Do SDG Funds Fulfil Their Promises?," ESMA, February 1, 2024, https://www.esma.europa.eu/sites/default/files/2024-02/ESMA50-524821-3098_TRV_article_-_Impact_investing_-_Do_SDG_funds_fulfil_their_promises.pdf.

14. Fredrik Dahlqvist et al., "Global Private Markets Report 2024: Private Markets in a Slower Era," McKinsey and Company, March 28, 2024, https://www.mckinsey.com/industries/private-capital/our-insights/global-private-markets-report-2024.

15. Dean Hand et al., *2023 GIINsight.*

16. "100% Forecasting Error Reduction and up to $300M Saving Potential for a Global High-Tech Hardware Leader," C3.ai, accessed August 27, 2024, https://c3.ai/customers/100-forecasting-error-reduction-and-up-to-300m-saving-potential-for-a-global-high-tech-hardware-leader/.

17. "C3 IoT," Rise Fund, accessed August 28, 2024, https://therisefund.com/portfolio/c3-iot.

18. Greg Brown et al., "Private Equity: Accomplishments and Challenges," *Journal of Applied Corporate Finance* 32, no. 3 (Summer 2020), https://doi.org/10.1111/jacf.12415.

19. Atul Gupta et al., "Owner Incentives and Performance in Healthcare: Private Equity Investment in Nursing Homes," *Review of Financial Studies* 37, no. 4 (2024): 1029–1077, https://doi.org/10.1093/rfs/hhad082.

20. Gupta, "Owner Incentives and Performance in Healthcare," 1052.

21. Brian Ayash and Mahdi Rastad, "Leveraged Buyouts and Financial Distress," *Finance Research Letters* 38 (January 2021), https://doi.org/10.1016/j.frl.2020.101452.

22. For a heartbreaking example of PE ownership of a major nursing home chain, leading eventually to the company's bankruptcy, see Peter Whoriskey and Dan Keating, "Overdoses, Bedsores, Broken Bones: What Happened When a Private-Equity Firm Sought to Care for Society's Most Vulnerable," *Washington Post*, November 25, 2018, https://www.washingtonpost.com/business/economy/opioid-overdoses-bedsores-and-broken-bones-what-happened-when-a-private-equity-firm-sought-profits-in-caring-for-societys-most-vulnerable/2018/11/25/09089a4a-ed14-11e8-baac-2a674e91502b_story.html.

23. William D. Cohan, "How Bono's Investment Partner Got Busted in the College-Admissions Scandal," *Vanity Fair*, May 2, 2019, https://www.vanityfair.com/news/2019/05/bonos-investment-partner-busted-in-the-college-admissions-scandal.

24. Patricia Hurtado, "Ex-TPG Star Bill McGlashan Gets Three Months in College Scam," Advisor Perspectives, May 31, 2021, https://www.advisorperspectives.com/articles/2021/05/13/ex-tpg-star-bill-mcglashan-gets-three-months-in-college-scam-1.

Chapter 15

1. Sasha Dichter et al., *60 Decibels Microfinance Index 2023* (60 Decibels, 2023), https://60decibels.com/wp-content/uploads/2023/09/60-Decibels-Microfinance-Index-Report-2023-5.pdf.

2. Mohammad Zainuddin and Ida Md. Yasin, "Are Women Better Borrowers in Microfinance? A Global Analysis," *Empirical Economics Letters* 19, no. 7 (July 2020): 651–660, https://papers.ssrn.com/sol3/papers.cfm?abstract_id=3669673.

3. My estimate from personal experience as a fund manager. See also, for example, "What's in a Microfinance Interest Rate," MicroVest, March 1, 2019, https://microvestfund.com/whats-in-a-microfinance-interest-rate/.

4. "Variations in Microcredit Interest Rates," CGAP, July 2008, https://www.cgap.org/sites/default/files/CGAP-Brief-Variations-in-Microcredit-Interest-Rates-Jul-2008.pdf.

5. Zainuddin and Yasin, "Are Women Better Borrowers."

6. Zainuddin and Yasin, "Are Women Better Borrowers."

7. "'Higher for Longer.' The New Interest Rate Regime and Its Implications for Microfinance," Enabling Qapital, November 3, 2023, https://enabling.ch/news/higher-for-longer-the-new-interest-rate-regime-and-its-implications-for-microfinance#.

8. US Government Accountability Office, *Microenterprise and Related Development Assistance: Challenges in Evaluating Lasting Benefits for Women and the Poor* (US Government Accountability Office, 2021), https://www.gao.gov/products/gao-21-328.

9. Rachael Meager, "Understanding the Average Impact of Microcredit Expansions: A Bayesian Hierarchical Analysis of Seven Randomized Experiments," *American Economics Journal: Applied Economics* 11, no. 1 (2019): 57–91, https://doi.org/10.1257/app.20170299.

10. Abhijit Banerjee et al., "The Miracle of Microfinance? Evidence from a Randomized Evaluation," *American Economics Journal: Applied Economics* 7, no. 1 (2015): 22–53, http://dx.doi.org/10.1257/app.20130533.

11. Pascaline Dupas and Jonathan Robinson, "Savings Constraints and Microenterprise Development: Evidence from a Field Experiment in Kenya," *American Economics Journal: Applied Economics* 5, no. 1 (2013): 163–192, http://dx.doi.org/10.1257/app.5.1.163.

Chapter 16

1. Gong Cheng et al., "Sovereign Green Bonds: A Catalyst for Sustainable Debt Market Development?," Working Paper No. 24/120 (International Monetary Fund, June 2024), https://www.imf.org/-/media/Files/Publications/WP/2024/English/wpiea2024120-print-pdf.ashx.

2. This assumes that the green project is not so large as to distort the underlying credit quality of the borrower, which is something the green bond issuer would normally want to avoid.

3. Quinn Curtis et al., "Green Bonds, Empty Promises," Working Paper (University of Virginia School of Law, February 2023), https://ssrn.com/abstract=4350209.

4. Miguel Almeida, *Sustainability-Linked Bonds: Building a High-Quality Market* (Climate Bonds Initiative, 2024), https://www.climatebonds.net/resources/reports/sustainability-linked-bonds-building-high-quality-market.

5. "Sustainability-Linked Bond of the Year: Republic of Chile," Environmental Finance, accessed September 5, 2024, https://www.environmental-finance.com/content/awards/environmental-finances-bond-awards-2023/winners/sustainability-linked-bond-of-the-year-republic-of-chile.html.

6. Almeida, *Sustainability-Linked Bonds*.

7. "Second Party Opinion: Itelyum," ISS ESG, September 10, 2021, https://www.iss-corporate.com/file/documents/spo/spo-20210910-Itelyum.pdf.

8. Alice Holian, "Dude, Where's My Coupon Step-Up?," 9fin, September 12, 2021, https://9fin.com/insights/dude-wheres-my-coupon-step-up.

9. "Stirling Square Capital Partners' Fourth Fund Invests in Itelyum in Partnership with Deutsche Beteiligungs AG," Stirling Square, August 16, 2021, https://www.stirlingsquare.com/news/itelyum.

10. Jim Parsons et al., "Impact Evaluation of the Adolescent Behavioral Learning Experience (ABLE) Program," Vera, September 2016, https://www.vera.org/publications/rikers-adolescent-behavioral-learning-experience-evaluation.

11. Zohen Khan et al., *Investment Research Report: The Bonds4Jobs Social Impact Bond* (Intellidex, 2021), https://www.researchgate.net/publication/351022616_Investment_research_report_The_Bonds4Jobs_social_impact_bond.

Chapter 17

1. Thomas Day et al., *Corporate Climate Responsibility Monitor 2022* (NewClimate Institute, 2022), https://newclimate.org/resources/publications/corporate-climate-responsibility-monitor-2022.

2. Victor Steenbergen and Abhishek Saurav, "The Effect of Multinational Enterprises on Climate Change," World Bank Group, May 23, 2023, https://thedocs.worldbank.org/en/doc/9a1339eeb35c11e262439bbda817a083-0430012023/original/MNEs-and-Climate-Change-summary-220523.pdf.

3. Maida Hadziosmanovik et al., "Update Trends Show Companies Are Ready for Scope 3 Reporting with US Climate Disclosure Rule," World Resources Institute, June 24, 2022, https://www.wri.org/update/trends-show-companies-are-ready-scope-3-reporting-us-climate-disclosure-rule.

4. "ExxonMobil Announces Ambition for Net Zero Greenhouse Gas Emissions by 2050," ExxonMobil, news release, January 18, 2022, https://corporate.exxonmobil.com/news/news-releases/2022/0118_exxonmobil-announces-ambition-for-net-zero-greenhouse-gas-emissions-by-2050#.

5. Parinitha Sastry, Emil Verner, and David Marques-Ibanez, "Business as Usual: Bank Net Zero Commitments, Lending and Engagement," May 22, 2024, VoxEU, https://cepr.org/voxeu/columns/business-usual-bank-net-zero-commitments-lending-and-engagement.

6. Saijel Kishan and Natasha White, "Wall Street's Top Banks Just Quit a Once Popular Alliance," Bloomberg, updated January 5, 2025, https://www.bloomberg.com

/news/articles/2025-01-04/wall-street-banks-keep-quitting-major-climate-alliance?embedded-checkout=true.

7. “Investment Trends and Outcomes in the Global Carbon Credit Market,” MSCI, September 13, 2023, https://www.msci.com/www/research-report/investment-trends-and-outcomes/04638716796.

8. Josh Gabbatiss, “Analysis: How Some of the World’s Largest Companies Rely on Carbon Offsets to ‘Reach Net Zero,’” Carbon Brief, September 27, 2023, https://interactive.carbonbrief.org/carbon-offsets-2023/companies.html.

9. “Too Many Cooks,” United Nations Climate Change, June 14, 2021, https://unfccc.int/news/too-many-cooks.

10. “A Vision for Clean Cooking Access for All,” International Energy Agency, July 2023, https://www.iea.org/reports/a-vision-for-clean-cooking-access-for-all/executive-summary.

11. “A Vision for Clean Cooking Access for All,” International Energy Agency.

12. Jennifer L., “Up in Smoke? Study Questions Accuracy of Cookstove Carbon Credits,” Carbon Credits, January 30, 2024, https://carboncredits.com/up-in-smoke-study-questions-accuracy-of-cookstove-carbon-credits/.

13. “A Comprehensive Quality Assessment of Cookstoves Carbon Credits,” Goldman School of Public Policy, accessed September 11, 2024, https://gspp.berkeley.edu/research-and-impact/centers/cepp/projects/berkeley-carbon-trading-project/cookstoves.

14. Chico Harlan, “How One Company’s Plan to Help the Planet Went Off the Rails,” *Washington Post*, September 1, 2024, https://www.washingtonpost.com/climate-environment/2024/08/24/carbon-credits-cook-stoves-africa/.

15. Patrick Greenfield, “Revealed: More than 90% of Rainforest Carbon Offsets by Biggest Certifier Are Worthless, Analysis Shows,” *Guardian*, January 18, 2023, https://www.theguardian.com/environment/2023/jan/18/revealed-forest-carbon-offsets-biggest-provider-worthless-verra-aoe.

16. Patrick Greenfield, “‘Nowhere Else to Go’: Forest Communities of Alto Mayo, Peru, at Centre of Offsetting Row,” *Guardian*, January 18, 2023, https://www.theguardian.com/environment/2023/jan/18/forest-communities-alto-mayo-peru-carbon-offsetting-aoe.

17. Ben Elgin, “A Top US Seller of Carbon Offsets Starts Investigating Its Own Projects,” Bloomberg, April 5, 2021, https://www.bloomberg.com/news/features/2021-04-05/a-top-u-s-seller-of-carbon-offsets-starts-investigating-its-own-projects.

18. Martin Cames et al., “How Additional Is the Clean Development Mechanism?,” Oko-Institut e.V., March 2016, https://climate.ec.europa.eu/system/files/2017-04/clean_dev_mechanism_en.pdf.

19. Fund information comes from their websites, accessed 3Q 2024. Overlap information comes from an online tool that ETF Research Center (https://www.etfrc.com/) makes available to compare fund holdings.

Chapter 18

1. "Climate Change Indicators: US Greenhouse Gas Emissions," Environmental Protection Agency, fig. 1, accessed September 13, 2024, https://www.epa.gov/climate-indicators/climate-change-indicators-us-greenhouse-gas-emissions.

2. "Fossil Fuel CO2 Emissions Increase Again in 2024," University of Reading, November 13, 2024, https://www.reading.ac.uk/news/2024/Research-News/Fossil-fuel-CO2-emissions-increase-again-in-2024#:~:text=With%20projected%20emissions%20from%20land,40.6%20billion%20tonnes%20last%20year.

3. "Post-COP 26 Snapshot," Net Zero Tracker, November 24, 2021, https://zerotracker.net/analysis/post-cop26-snapshot.

4. "Annual Greenhouse Gas Emissions Including Land Use," Our World in Data, accessed February 6, 2025, https://ourworldindata.org/grapher/ghg-emissions-by-world-region.

5. CO_2 emissions by fuel: Hannah Ritchie, Pablo Rosado, and Max Roser, "CO_2 Emissions by Fuel," Our World in Data, updated January 2024, https://ourworldindata.org/emissions-by-fuel. Total GHG emissions: "Historical GHG Emissions," Climate Watch, accessed September 13, 2024, https://www.climatewatchdata.org/ghg-emissions?breakBy=sector&end_year=2021&start_year=1990.

6. "Energy Explained: Your Guide to Understanding Energy," US Energy Information Administration, accessed September 13, 2024, https://www.eia.gov/energyexplained/.

7. Maxine Joselow, "Republicans Want to Plant a Trillion Trees. Scientists Are Skeptical," *Washington Post*, August 2, 2023, https://www.washingtonpost.com/climate-environment/2023/08/02/trillion-trees-republicans-climate/.

8. Sissi Cao, "Bill Gates Says Planting Trees to Solve Climate Crisis Is 'Complete Nonsense,'" Observer, September 21, 2023.

9. "If Every Energy Transition Is Different, Which Course Will Accelerate Yours?," EY, accessed September 12, 2024, https://web.archive.org/web/20231216093824/https://assets.ey.com/content/dam/ey-sites/ey-com/en_gl/topics/energy/ey-energy-and-resources-transition-acceleration.pdf.

10. Barbara Buchner et al., "Global Landscape of Climate Finance 2023," Climate Policy Initiative, November 2023, https://www.climatepolicyinitiative.org/wp-content/uploads/2023/11/Global-Landscape-of-Climate-Finance-2023.pdf.

11. John E. T. Bistline et al., "Economic Implications of the Climate Provisions of the Inflation Reduction Act," *Brookings Papers on Economic Activity* (Spring 2023): 77–157, https://www.brookings.edu/wp-content/uploads/2023/03/BPEA_Spring2023_Bistline-et-al_unembargoedUpdated.pdf.

12. Robert Armstrong, "Warren Buffett on Why Companies Cannot be Moral Arbiters," *Financial Times*, December 29, 2019, https://www.ft.com/content/ebbc9b46-1754-11ea-9ee4-11f260415385.

13. Armstrong, "Warren Buffett"; emphasis added.

14. "Greenhouse Gas Reduction Fund: Charge to EFAB on Private Capital Mobilization," Environmental Protection Agency, April 2024, https://www.epa.gov/system/files/documents/2024-04/ggrf-charge-discussion-to-efab-capital-mobilization.pdf.

15. Kevin Buehler et al., "Delivering Impact from US Green Bank Financing," McKinsey, April 20, 2023, https://www.mckinsey.com/capabilities/sustainability/our-insights/delivering-impact-from-us-green-bank-financing.

16. "Carbon Taxation in Sweden," Sweden Ministry of Finance, March 2023, https://www.government.se/contentassets/419cb2cafa93423c891c09cb9914801b/230323-carbon-tax-sweden---general-info.pdf.

17. Data download: "Sweden GDP Growth Rate 1960–2024," Macrotrends, accessed September 13, 2024, https://www.macrotrends.net/global-metrics/countries/SWE/sweden/gdp-growth-rate.

18. Gilbert E. Metcalf and James H. Stock, "Measuring the Macroeconomic Impact of Carbon Taxes," *AEA Papers and Proceedings* 110 (May 2020): 101–106, https://www.aeaweb.org/articles?id=10.1257/pandp.20201081.

19. "Carbon Tax Countries 2024," World Population Review, accessed September 13, 2024, https://worldpopulationreview.com/country-rankings/carbon-tax-countries.

20. Ian W. H. Parry et al., "Still Not Getting Energy Prices Right: A Global and Country Update of Fossil Fuel Subsidies," Working Paper No. 2021/236 (International Monetary Fund, September 2021), 13, https://www.imf.org/en/Publications/WP/Issues/2021/09/23/Still-Not-Getting-Energy-Prices-Right-A-Global-and-Country-Update-of-Fossil-Fuel-Subsidies-466004.

21. "How Carbon Prices Are Taking Over the World," *The Economist*, October 1, 2023, https://www.economist.com/finance-and-economics/2023/10/01/how-carbon-prices-are-taking-over-the-world.

22. Adam Wilson and Tony Lenoir, "US Renewable Energy Credit Market Size Forecast to Approach $40B by 2033," February 13, 2024, S&P Global Marketing Intelligence, https://www.spglobal.com/market-intelligence/en/news-insights/research/us-renewable-energy-credit-market-size-forecast-to-approach-40b-by-2033.

23. “Regional Greenhouse Gast Initiative: Findings and Recommendations for the Third Program Review,” Acadia Center, April 2023, https://acadiacenter.wpengine-powered.com/wp-content/uploads/2023/04/AC_RGGI_2023_Layout_R6.pdf.

24. “California Cap and trade,” Center for Climate and Energy Solutions, accessed October 4, 2024, https://www.c2es.org/content/california-cap-and-trade/.

Conclusion

1. Jennifer Sherer and Elise Gould, “Data Show Anti-Union ‘Right-to-Work’ Laws Damage State Economies,” *Working Economics Blog* (Economic Policy Institute), February 13, 2024, https://www.epi.org/blog/data-show-anti-union-right-to-work-laws-damage-state-economies-as-michigans-repeal-takes-effect-new-hampshire-should-continue-to-reject-right-to-work-legislation/.

2. Karla Walter and David Madland, “8 Ways the Biden Administration Has Fought for Working People by Strengthening Unions,” Center for American Progress, December 19, 2023, https://www.americanprogressaction.org/article/8-ways-the-biden-administration-has-fought-for-working-people-by-strengthening-unions/.

3. Elizabeth B. Wydra et al, “Wilcox v. Trump,” Rule of Law, Constitutional Accountability Center, accessed June 8, 2025, https://www.theusconstitution.org/litigation/wilcox-v-trump/.

4. “Corporate Legal Accountability Annual Briefing 2019—The Future of Work: Litigating Labour Relationships in the Gig Economy,” Business & Human Rights Resource Centre, March 25, 2019, https://www.business-humanrights.org/en/from-us/briefings/the-future-of-work-litigating-labour-relationships-in-the-gig-economy/; “Real and Nominal Value of the Federal Minimum Wage in the United States from 1938 to 2024,” Statista, July 26, 2024, https://www.statista.com/statistics/1065466/real-nominal-value-minimum-wage-us/#:~:text=When%20adjusted%20for%20inflation%2C%20the,increases%20to%2013.05%20U.S.%20dollars; Matthew A. Sloan et al, “Radical Change at OSHA During Second Trump Administration?” Seyfarth Shaw LLP, December 4, 2024, https://www.environmentalsafetyupdate.com/2024/12/radical-change-at-osha-during-second-trump-administration/.

5. Denise Hearn, “Harms from Concentrated Industries: A Primer,” Columbia Center on Sustainable Investment, February 2024, https://ccsi.columbia.edu/sites/default/files/content/docs/ccsi-harms-from-concentrated-industries.pdf?ref=embodied-economics.ghost.io.

6. “The World’s Largest 500 Asset Managers,” Thinking Ahead Institute, October 2023, https://www.thinkingaheadinstitute.org/content/uploads/2023/10/PI-500-2023-1.pdf.

7. Graham Steele, “The New Money Trust: How Large Money Managers Control Our Economy and What We Can Do About It,” American Economic Liberties Project,

November 2020, 5, https://www.economicliberties.us/wp-content/uploads/2020/11/Working-Paper-Series-on-Corporate-Power_8_FINAL.pdf.

8. Dan Morenoff, "Break Up the ESG Investing Giants," *Wall Street Journal*, August 31, 2022, https://www.wsj.com/articles/break-up-the-esg-investing-giants-state-street-blackrock-vanguard-voting-ownership-big-three-competitor-antitrust-11661961693.

9. Morenoff, "Break Up the ESG Investing Giants."

10. This was one of the key points in a January 2025 ruling by a federal judge that found that a pension plan was overly influenced by one of its fund managers. See Joshua A. Lichtenstein et al., "Practical Takeaways from *Spence v. American Airlines, Inc.* for ERISA Plan Fiduciaries," Ropes & Gray, January 15, 2025, https://www.ropesgray.com/en/insights/alerts/2025/01/practical-takeaways-from-spence-v-american-airlines-inc-for-erisa-plan-fiduciaries.

11. "Active vs. Passive Funds by Investment Category," Morningstar, updated September 23, 2024, https://www.morningstar.com/business/insights/blog/funds/active-vs-passive-investing.

12. "Empowering Investors Through Voting Choice," BlackRock, accessed February 8, 2025, https://www.blackrock.com/corporate/about-us/investment-stewardship/blackrock-voting-choice#:~:text=BlackRock%20Voting%20Choice%20is%20a,as%20pass%2Dthrough%20voting%5D; "Voting Choice-Voting Policy Comparison," BlackRock, July 2024, https://www.blackrock.com/corporate/literature/publication/voting-choice-voting-policy-comparison.pdf.

13. Benjamin Braun, "Exit, Control, and Politics: Structural Power and Corporate Governance Under Asset Manager Capitalism," *Politics & Society* 50, no. 4 (2022): 630–654, https://journals.sagepub.com/doi/epub/10.1177/00323292221126262.

14. Michael B. Dorff, *Becoming a Public Benefit Corporation: Express Your Values, Energize Stakeholders, Make the World a Better Place* (Stanford Business Books, 2023).

15. Jill E. Fisch and Stephen Davidoff Solomon, "The 'Value' of a Public Benefit Corporation," Working Paper No. 585/2021 (European Corporate Governance Institute, May 2021), https://www.ecgi.global/sites/default/files/working_papers/documents/fischsolomonfinal_1.pdf.

16. Ruth Jin, "The Development of Delaware Public Benefit Corporations and Their Access to Capital," American Bar Association, April 21, 2023, https://www.americanbar.org/groups/business_law/resources/newsletters/delaware-public-benefit-corporations/.

17. "Warby Parker," Good on You sustainability rating, accessed February 10, 2025, https://directory.goodonyou.eco/brand/warby-parker.

18. Jason Blevins, "B Corp Gets an A+," Park 360, June 28, 2018, https://adventureparkinsider.com/b-corp-gets-an-a/.

19. Anjli Raval, "The Struggle for the Soul of the B Corp Movement," *Financial Times*, February 19, 2023, https://www.ft.com/content/0b632709-afda-4bdc-a6f3-bb0b02eb5a62.

20. "The B Corp Standard Is at Risk," Fair World Project, June 15, 2022, https://fairworldproject.org/the-b-corp-standard-is-at-risk/.

21. "Nespresso Global," B Lab, accessed February 10, 2025, https://www.bcorporation.net/en-us/find-a-b-corp/company/nespresso-global/.

22. Lynn Stout, *The Shareholder Value Myth* (Berrett-Koehler Publishers, 2012), 31.

23. Rebecca Burton, "2023 Pay Trends," WTW, December 18, 2023, https://www.wtwco.com/en-us/insights/2023/12/2023-us-director-pay-trends.

24. Burton, "2023 Pay Trends."

25. Paul Washington and Merel Spierings, "Making Board Refreshment a Reality," The Conference Board, March 9, 2023, https://www.conference-board.org/publications/making-board-refreshment-a-reality-op-ed.

26. Laurent Belsie, "Worker Representation on Company Boards Raises Investment," *The Digest*, February 1, 2020, https://www.nber.org/digest/feb20/worker-representation-company-boards-raises-investment.

27. Robert Scholz and Sigurt Vitols, "Board-Level Codetermination: A Driving Force for Corporate Social Responsibility in German Companies?," *European Journal of Industrial Relations* 25, no. 3 (2019), https://doi.org/10.1177/09596801198305.

Index